THE MESSIAH FACTOR

THE

MESSIAH

FACTOR

TONY PEARCE

Lighthouse Trails Publishing
Eureka, Montana

The Messiah Factor
©2004, 2017 Tony Pearce
First and Second Editions 2004, 2010 New Wine Press (UK)
Third Edition 2017 Lighthouse Trails Publishing
(see back of book for publisher and author contact information)
All rights reserved. No part of this book may be reproduced, stored in
a retrieval system, or transmitted in any form by any means, whether
electronic, mechanical, photocopying, recordings, or otherwise without
prior written permission from the publisher. Excerpts and quotes may
be used without permission as the US Fair Use Act allows. Scripture
quotations are taken from the *King James Version*. Cover design by
Light for the Last Days; cover photo from bigstockphoto.com; used
with permission. For all photo credits see page 202.

Library of Congress Cataloging-in-Publication Data

Names: Pearce, Tony, 1946- author.
Title: The Messiah factor / Tony Pearce.
Description: Third edition. | Eureka, Montana : Lighthouse Trails
   Publishing, [2017] | First edition 2010, New Wine Press | Includes
   bibliographical references and index.
Identifiers: LCCN 2017031311 | ISBN 9781942423263 (softbound :
alk. paper)
Subjects: LCSH: Messiah. | Jesus Christ--Messiahship. | Jesus Christ--Jewish
   interpretation. | Messiah--Judaism. | God--Biblical teachings. |
   Christianity--Relations--Judaism. | Judaism--Relations--Christianity. |
   Bible--Criticism, interpretation, etc. | Rabbinical literature--History
   and criticism.
Classification: LCC BL475 .P43 2017 | DDC 232/.1--dc23 LC record
available at https://lccn.loc.gov/2017031311

Note: Lighthouse Trails Publishing books are available at special quantity
discounts. Contact information for publisher in back of book.

Printed in the United States of America

Dedication

This book is written with very grateful thanks to Nikki, my first wife, who helped me in this ministry until she went to be with the Lord in 1998 and to Barbara, my second wife, who helps me carry it on.

Also by Tony Pearce

Countdown to Calamity: Current events in light of Biblical Prophecy

Who Really Killed Jesus?

Messiah, Israel, and the End Days

What is the World Heading For?

The Da Vinci Code

The Omega Course

MAGAZINES

Light for the Last Days

Alpha & Omega

CONTENTS

1/Who Do You Say That I Am?   9

2/Who Killed Jesus?   13

3/Out of Night   25

4/So What About the Messiah?   37

5/Messiah—A Great Man Or a Divine Person?   47

6/Can We Believe in the Virgin Birth?   65

7/The Suffering Servant   83

8/"When I See the Blood"   99

9/The Fall of the Second Temple   109

10/No Peace—No Messiah   121

11/Is Torah the Bridge to God?   141

12/The Messiah and the End of Days   161

Appendix: Messianic Prophecies   181

Endnotes   197

Photo Credits   202

Index   203

CHAPTER 1

WHO DO YOU SAY THAT I AM?

———◆———

CAESAREA PHILIPPI

December 27th 1979. I was visiting Israel for the first time with my late wife, Nikki, and my daughter, Rachel. We were being shown around by friends who lived at Stella Carmel, near Haifa. As we traveled through this ancient, modern land, we felt an amazing sense of destiny and excitement, seeing not just places where things had happened in the past, but where they are happening now. On this particular day, we went as far north as we could go and reached a place called Baneas in the foothills of the Golan Heights.

The main feature of the place was a shrine to the Greek god Pan and an association with the New Testament. Here was the site of Caesarea Philippi, the Roman settlement where Jesus came with His disciples and asked them a very significant question: *"Who do you say that I am?"*

As we climbed up to the shrine to Pan, I looked upon the heights above which looked grim and forbidding. I thought of the life and death battles that had been fought between the Israelis and the Syrians there in the wars of 1967 and 1973. I thought of the Israeli soldiers now on duty looking to the hills from where war and destruction had come in recent memory. I thought of the nearby border with Lebanon and the civil war raging there at that time claiming thousands of lives.

Beyond that, I thought of the news which was just coming through of the Soviet invasion of Afghanistan, not knowing that these events would, in time, contribute to the collapse of the Soviet Union, the rise of Islamic terrorism through the Taliban and Al-Qaeda, and the global "War on Terrorism."

At Baneas, the Greeks had placed a shrine to Pan, the god of nature from whence we get the term *pantheism*, the belief popularized today through the New Age movement that God is to be found in everything (the trees, the earth, people, and animals) and that we are all part of one interconnected whole linking us up to the divine. At the same place (Caesarea Philippi), Jesus, the Jew, had asked the question that cuts through the fog of human philosophy and has a vital relevance to all people of the Earth, especially those living today in the region where He first posed it.

Who do you say that I am? Is the answer a prophet, a good man, a deceiver, the one we follow, or the one we despise? Or is it Peter's answer in the Gospel, "Thou art the Christ, the Son of the living God" (Matthew 16:16)?

There is a special relevance to this question for the two peoples locked in conflict over this land, the Jews and the Arabs. The dominant religions of both peoples, Judaism and Islam, believe that God is one, an absolute unity whose nature rules out the Christian idea of God as a plural unity of Father, Son, and Holy Spirit. Both reject the idea that Jesus is the mediator, the one who reconciles us to God and one another. But both need a mediator to reconcile them in their bitter struggle for the land of Israel. However, the Jews have in their favor Scripture which reveals from the beginning that God refers to Himself as One God and also as "us" (Genesis 1:26).

JERUSALEM

One week later we were in Jerusalem. We visited holy places including synagogues, churches, mosques, Yad va Shem (the Holocaust memorial museum), and Mea Sharim (the ultra-Orthodox Jewish quarter). Then, on the last day of our visit, we went to Gethsemane, the place where Jesus was arrested. From there, we walked a little way down the Kidron Valley.

It was Friday afternoon, and we wanted to go to the Western (Wailing) Wall to watch the Sabbath celebrations begin. I noticed a footpath, which, according to our map, would be a short cut to where we wanted to go. I left Nikki and Rachel in the valley below to investigate it. As I climbed up a narrow ridge, I realized this was a very foolish thing to do. Two Arab boys ran down from the Muslim cemetery above me and stood on either side of me demanding my money and threatening to push me down the ridge. I gave them the money, and they ran off laughing at me.

I ran after them, shaking my fist in anger and fear. I was relieved to find Nikki and Rachel safe in the valley below and told them what had happened. As we walked down the valley, I was feeling angry with the boys who had robbed me, when suddenly it struck me where I was. This was the path where the soldiers would have taken Jesus on the way to the High Priest Caiaphas' house on the night He was arrested. I thought of Him walking this path nearly 2000 years ago and knew He was saying to me, "Forgive them, pray for them, love them."

We walked through the alleys of the Old City and made our way to the Western Wall. It was late Friday afternoon, and from the Al Aqsa mosque above us, the muezzin was calling the Muslims to prayer. Before us, crowds of Jewish men were gathering in front of the Wall. They began dancing and singing joyfully to God.

Suddenly, it dawned on me what was actually happening in the scene before me. Here were two groups of people, Jews and Muslims, praying fervently to God as they understood him. Both believe that God is One. Both strongly deny that Jesus, as understood in the New Testament, is either the Messiah or the Son of God. Physically, they were very close to each other. Spiritually, they were a million miles apart, divided by a great wall of hostility and fear of each other.

Here they were, praying, and what was there between them? A massive wall, the Western Wall.

At that moment, I felt that the Lord was saying to me, "You haven't prayed for those Arab boys yet." So I began to pray that God would forgive the boys who had robbed me, and then I began to pray about the division between the Jewish and Arab people.

**A Group of Orthodox Jews Dancing at the
Western Wall in Jerusalem—2015**

As I did so, I pictured Jesus breaking down that Wall and reaching out one hand to the Jewish people and one hand to the Arabs saying, "I love you, I am the one who can reconcile you to God and to each other. I am the one mediator between God and all human beings. Today, I am offering you peace with God, a new start, and a glorious future; but I tell you with weeping that outside of me, there is no peace, there is only calamity coming, bloodshed, lives ruined, and cities destroyed, armies of the world gathering for the final conflict. Today, you must make your choice. Who do you say that I am?"

Chapter 2

WHO KILLED JESUS?

———◆———

Sadly, for millions of Jewish people, the idea that Jesus could be the one to bring peace and reconciliation seems ridiculous and offensive.

Nikki used to visit a Jewish lady who was born around the beginning of the 20th century and brought up in a small town in Poland. Her first memory of the name of Jesus was when her parents told her to hide in a cupboard in their home because it was "Good Friday," and on that day, the Roman Catholics would come out of their church services into the Jewish quarter to throw stones at the Jews "to avenge the death of Jesus." Not surprisingly, it was hard for her to see Jesus as anyone who had an answer to anything. As far as she was concerned, Jesus was "someone who hated us and is responsible for our misery."

The roots of this hatred toward the Jews go back a long way. John Chrysostom, considered a saint and church father who lived in the fourth century, wrote:

> The Jews are the most worthless of all men. They are lecherous, greedy and rapacious. They are perfidious murderers of Christ. The Jews are the odious assassins of Christ and for

killing God there is no expiation possible, no indulgence or pardon. Christians may never cease vengeance and the Jews must live in servitude forever. God always hated the Jews. It is incumbent upon Christians to hate Jews.[1]

When Constantine established Christianity as the official religion of the Roman Empire in 312, he issued many anti-Jewish laws. Jews were forbidden to accept converts, while every enticement was used to make them forsake Judaism. At the Council of Nicaea in 325, he said, "It is right to demand what our reason approves and that we should have nothing in common with the Jews."

As Christianity in its Roman Catholic form became the dominant religion of Europe, those who rejected it were considered to be the forces of antichrist. The main group of rejectors were the Jewish people who, therefore, were considered by the church to be the "anti-Christ" and thus suffered continual persecution. In Spain in 613, all Jews who refused to be baptized had to leave the country. A few years later the remaining Jews were dispossessed and given to wealthy "pious" Christians as slaves.

The first Crusade in 1096 saw fierce persecution of Jewish communities as the Crusaders began their journeys to the "Holy Land" to "liberate" it from the Muslims. They said, "We are going to fight Christ's enemies in Palestine (i.e. the Muslims), but should we forget his enemies in our midst (i.e. the Jews)?" Twelve thousand Jews were killed in the cities along the River Rhine alone. When the Roman Catholic Crusaders captured Jerusalem in 1099, they massacred all the Jews and Muslims they could find.

In 1208, Pope Innocent III condemned the Jews to eternal slavery by decreeing:

> [T]he Jews, against whom the blood of Jesus Christ calls out, although they ought not to be killed, lest the Christian people forget the Divine Law, yet as wanderers ought they remain upon the earth until their countenance be filled with shame.[2]

The first ritual-murder charge against the Jewish community was in Norwich in 1144 when the Jews were accused of killing a Christian child at Passover time to drain his blood in order to make Passover matzos. This hideous and ridiculous charge has resurfaced time and again, most recently in the Muslim world, leading to massacres of the Jews. In 1290, King Edward I expelled all Jews from England.

In 1478, the Spanish Inquisition was directed against heretics—Jews and non-Catholic Christians. In 1492, Jews were given the choice of forced baptism or expulsion from Spain. Three hundred thousand left the country penniless.

Martin Luther hoped initially that he would attract Jews to his Protestant faith, understanding that they could not accept the superstitions and persecutions of Rome. But when they rejected his attempts to convert them, he turned on them and uttered words of hatred, later used word for word by the Nazis in their propaganda:

> What shall we Christians do with this damned, rejected race of the Jews? First their synagogues should be set on fire. Secondly their homes should likewise be broken down and destroyed. Thirdly they should be deprived of their prayer books and Talmuds. Fourthly their rabbis must be forbidden under threat of death to teach any more. Fifthly passport and traveling privileges should be absolutely forbidden to the Jews. Sixthly they ought to be stopped from usury. Seventhly let the young and strong Jews and Jewesses be given the flail, the axe, the spade, the distaff, and spindle and let them earn their bread by the sweat of their noses. To sum up, dear princes and nobles who have Jews in your domains, if this advice of mine does not suit you, then find a better one, so that you and we may all be free of this insufferable devilish burden—the Jews.[3]

In the late 19th century, the Russian Orthodox Church instigated the pogroms, violent attacks on Jewish communities of the kind portrayed in the film *Fiddler on the Roof.* They devised a solution to the "Jewish problem"—one third extermination, one third forcible conversion to Christianity, and one third expulsion.

Russian anti-Semites produced the libelous pamphlet, *The Protocols of the Elders of Zion*, alleging a Jewish conspiracy to take over the world. This fiction was treated as a proven fact by the Nazis and was part of their propaganda effort to prepare people for the "Final Solution," the extermination of six million members of European Jewry in the ovens of the Holocaust. Today, the same libel is being peddled in the Muslim world to whip up hatred for Israel and the Jewish people.

This brief history of Jewish suffering shows the terrible truth that most of it has been instigated by people who claimed to be Christians. The main accusation that has been brought against the Jewish people by the professing church is that "the Jews killed Jesus."

WHO SAYS THE JEWS KILLED JESUS?

Back in 1978, I was working as a French teacher at the Hasmonean School, an Orthodox Jewish grammar school in north London. One day, I was covering for an absent teacher, minding my own business while the class got on with their work. One of the boys put his hand up and said, "Please sir, I want to ask you something. You're a Christian. Why do you Christians say we killed Jesus?"

I answered him as best I could, saying that I personally did not say this, but agreed that much of the professing church had done so because they did not really understand the faith they claimed to represent or who Jesus really was. This let loose an outburst of questions and comments from the boys on what was obviously an explosive issue to them. News of this discussion got back to the Rabbis in the school, and the next day one of them came to me and said, "Mr. Pearce, we know you are a sincere Christian and are friendly to our people, but please do not mention the founder of Christianity again in this school."

As I prayed about it afterwards, I realized how much hurt there is in the hearts of Jewish people over the way they have been persecuted in the name of Jesus. I also became aware of how much deeper is Jesus' own hurt over the cruel misrepresentation which has been given to the

Jewish people by His supposed followers down through the centuries, leading to a massive wall coming between Him and His own people.

The very first verse of the New Testament tells us of "the generation of Jesus Christ, the son of David, the son of Abraham" (Matthew 1:1). Throughout the New Testament, Jesus' identity as a Jew is stressed and given special significance in that the Jewish people were singularly picked out to be the bearers of God's laws and God's covenant. Jesus was circumcised on the eighth day (Luke 2:21), brought up in an observant Jewish home (Luke 2:41), and learned the Torah* from His youth (Luke 2:46-49).

He told a Samaritan woman that "salvation is of the Jews" (John 4:22), and He kept the Jewish feasts (John 7:2, John 10:22). He told His disciples in their first preaching mission not to go to the Gentiles, "but go rather to the lost sheep of the house of Israel" (Matthew 10:6). Sure, He had fierce controversies with the religious leaders of His day, but so did the Hebrew prophets—Isaiah, Jeremiah, Amos, and others.

Concerning the crucifixion, the New Testament does not put the blame on "the Jews" and certainly never even hints that succeeding generations of Jews should be persecuted on account of it. Some believe there is a problem with John's Gospel in its use of the term "the Jews" to describe the opposition to Jesus, but an intelligent reading of the text shows that John is talking of the Jewish religious leadership, not the entire Jewish people. John 5:18 states:

> Therefore the Jews sought the more to kill him, because he not only had broken the sabbath, but said also that God was his Father, making himself equal with God.

Obviously, because Jesus Himself and His followers were Jewish, this cannot be referring to the entire Jewish population.

In many ways, the Book of John is the most Jewish of the four Gospels, showing the connection between Jesus' teaching and Jewish

---

*Torah—the first five books of the Bible, also known as the Pentateuch. Considered by Judaism to be the most important section of the Bible and read in its entirety in the Synagogue every year.

festivals and customs. Yet, in the same Gospel, Jesus makes it very clear that the Jews are not to be blamed for His ensuing death.

> Therefore doth my Father love me, because I lay down my life, that I might take it again. No man taketh it from me, but I lay it down of myself. I have power to lay it down, and I have power to take it again. This commandment have I received of my Father. (John 10:17-18)

The implication of this is clear. Jesus Himself takes responsibility for His own death.* Jesus' death happens at the time and manner of His choosing in order that He might fulfill the Father's will by dying as the sacrifice for the sins of the world and rising again from the dead to give eternal life to those who receive Him. No human being, Jewish or Gentile, has the right or the power to take Jesus' life from Him against His will. This fulfills the prophecy of Isaiah 53, which states concerning the sufferings of the Messiah:

> [I]t pleased the LORD to bruise him; he hath put him to grief. (Isaiah 53: 10)

In chapter seven of this book, we will look at the different arguments about this prophecy, but taking the view that it is about the sacrificial death of Messiah, the responsibility for Messiah's sufferings is placed on God Himself. "It pleased the LORD to bruise him" means that Jesus was put to death to fulfill the will of God.

---

*And because Jesus died for the sins of the whole world, not only is the entire human race "responsible" for Jesus' crucifixion, but the very sins of hatred, persecution, and extermination of the Jews are among the sins that nailed Jesus to the Cross. It is therefore extremely hypocritical to blame the Jewish people for nailing Jesus to the Cross when in truth it is we who have done it. That is why we read in Zechariah 2:8 that whoever touches the Jews touches the apple of God's eye.

The Gospels take up this idea as we see Jesus submitting Himself to the will of God in order to redeem the world. He prayed in Gethsemane:

> O my Father, if it be possible, let this cup pass from me: nevertheless not as I will, but as thou wilt. (Matthew 26:39)

"This cup" refers to the suffering which He knew lay ahead. It was necessary for Him to go through this suffering in order that He might be "the Lamb of God, which taketh away the sin of the world" (John 1:29).

According to the Book of Hebrews, we are invited to come to "Jesus the mediator of the new covenant, and to the blood of sprinkling, that speaketh better things than that of Abel" (Hebrews 12:24). The blood of Abel spoke of vengeance for Cain's sin of murder (Genesis 4), but the blood of Jesus speaks of mercy and forgiveness.

Wrong church teaching, however, has turned this on its head and used the verse in Matthew's Gospel, "His blood be on us, and on our children" (Matthew 27:25), to claim that the suffering of the Jewish people is the result of a self-inflicted curse and even that Christians are, therefore, justified in persecuting the Jewish people in Jesus' name.

Nothing could be further from the truth. Jesus Himself prayed from the Cross, "Father, forgive them; for they know not what they do" (Luke 23:34), thus expressing God's will that even those immediately responsible for the death of Jesus, whether Jewish or Gentile (Roman), should be able to find forgiveness through His name. Do we base our theology on the words of an emotionally enraged crowd or on the sound words of the Lord Jesus?

The answer to Jesus' prayer was to be found not long afterwards through the preaching of the apostles. Peter *did* place human responsibility for the death of Jesus on those who had called for Him to be crucified:

> The God of Abraham, and of Isaac, and of Jacob, the God of our fathers, hath glorified his Son Jesus; whom ye delivered

up, and denied him in the presence of Pilate, when he was determined to let him go. But ye denied the Holy One and the Just, and desired a murderer to be granted unto you; and killed the Prince of life, whom God hath raised from the dead; whereof we are witnesses. (Acts 3:13-15)

This was not to say that every Jew alive was responsible for the actual betrayal of Jesus to the Roman authorities because Peter himself was Jewish, as were all the followers of Jesus at that time. And it was certainly not to say that subsequent generations of Jews, who had no connection with the decision to call for Jesus' death, were responsible. It was to say there were people alive, who were actually listening to Peter speak at that very moment, who were directly responsible.

But even to them, there was a message of hope and forgiveness. Explaining the meaning of the death and resurrection of Jesus, Peter said:

And now, brethren, I wot that through ignorance ye did it, as did also your rulers. But those things, which God before had shewed by the mouth of all his prophets, that Christ should suffer, he hath so fulfilled. Repent ye therefore, and be converted, that your sins may be blotted out, when the times of refreshing shall come from the presence of the Lord. (Acts 3:17-19)

The people who called for the death of Jesus were responsible for the miscarriage of justice that took place. However, they were ignorant of the spiritual meaning of it, hence Jesus' words, "they know not what they do." The purpose of the preaching of the apostles was to tell them why Jesus died and rose again and to show them how they too could find forgiveness and eternal salvation by repenting of their sin and believing in His name.

But the fact remains that while Jesus' death on the Cross paid for the sins of those directly responsible for His crucifixion, His death covered the sins of all of the human race—both Jew and Gentile. It is clear that the message of the Gospel was, from the beginning, intended to be "the power of God unto salvation to every one that believeth; to the Jew first, and also to the Greek [Gentile]" (Romans 1:16).

Both Jews and Gentiles had to make a choice, whether to believe in the salvation offered by the Messiah or to reject it. Of course, many Jewish people did reject the apostles' message, exactly as it happens today when the same message is proclaimed throughout the world to all races and cultures. There was a division amongst the Jews of Jesus' day between those who were for Him and those who were against Him; and this exact same division takes place today throughout the world, wherever the Gospel is preached.

The statement which really tells us who was responsible for the death of Jesus is to be found in Acts, chapter four:

> [The apostles] lifted up their voice to God with one accord, and said, Lord, thou art God, which hast made heaven, and earth, and the sea, and all that in them is: Who by the mouth of thy servant David hast said, Why did the heathen rage, and the people imagine vain things? The kings of the earth stood up, and the rulers were gathered together against the Lord, and against his Christ. For of a truth against thy holy child Jesus, whom thou hast anointed, both Herod, and Pontius Pilate, with the Gentiles, and the people of Israel, were gathered together, For to do whatsoever thy hand and thy counsel determined before to be done. (Acts 4:24-28)

In this prayer, all categories of people are implicated—Herod and Pontius Pilate with the Gentiles and the people of Israel. The Gentiles are actually mentioned before the people of Israel; therefore, they have no right to claim any superiority or judgmental attitude toward the Jews. It is clear that the physical act of crucifying Jesus was carried out on the orders of the Roman governor by Roman soldiers in the Roman way. Strangely, no one has ever suggested that the Italians killed Jesus and should be placed under a curse because of this!

All this happened "to do whatsoever thy hand and thy counsel determined before to be done"; in other words, to fulfill the predetermined plan of God. So again, the ultimate responsibility for the death of Jesus rests with God Himself in order to fulfill His purposes.

Any persecution of the Jews by the churches is a terrible distortion of the truth and a betrayal of the real Messiah Jesus. Unfortunately, the church did the exact opposite of what Paul taught in his letter to the Romans, where he spoke of Israel and the Jewish people being the root which supports the "olive tree." By this he meant that the Christian faith is based on the revelation given to the world through the Jewish people in the Jewish Bible and fulfilled in the Jewish Messiah. His message has been communicated to the Gentiles by His Jewish disciples who wrote the New Testament. Therefore, if Christians want to have true spiritual life, they have to acknowledge the debt they have to Israel and to repay that debt with love for the Jewish people.

Paul even argued that the fact that the majority of Jewish people had not accepted Jesus as Messiah had benefited the Gentiles and that, as a result, Gentile Christians should do what they can to make their faith attractive to Jewish people:

> I say then, Have they stumbled that they should fall? God forbid: but rather through their fall salvation is come unto the Gentiles, for to provoke them to jealousy. Now if the fall of them be the riches of the world, and the diminishing of them the riches of the Gentiles; how much more their fulness? For I speak to you Gentiles, inasmuch as I am the apostle of the Gentiles, I magnify mine office: if by any means I may provoke to emulation them which are my flesh, and might save some of them. (Romans 11:11-14)

Paul goes on to make it clear that whether the Jewish people accept Jesus or not, they are still "beloved for the fathers' sakes" (i.e. the patriarchs of Israel and the covenant God made with them) because "the gifts and calling of God are without repentance [irrevocable]" (Romans 11:28-29). On this basis, Christians have a responsibility to love the Jewish people and treat them with justice and kindness, no matter what they believe about Jesus. Significantly, Paul wrote this letter to Christians living in Rome, the capital of the Roman Empire and the city which was to dominate Christendom in the following centuries.

What went wrong? As the church became dominated by large numbers of Gentiles joining it, Jewish believers in Jesus became a minority. The Christians began to move away from the pattern of living given them by Jesus and the apostles, forming a religious institution which bore little resemblance to the original model given in the New Testament. They also wanted to ingratiate themselves with the Roman authorities who were hostile to the Jewish people following the failed Jewish revolts against Rome in 70 and 135. Following the fall of the Roman Empire, Roman Catholicism emerged as the dominant force in Europe, and the Bishop of Rome became the Pope, taking on much of the power and character of the Roman Emperor (even one of his titles—Pontifex Maximus). This produced a tragic distortion of the Christian message dominated by a corrupted clergy with vast wealth at its disposal, exploiting and corrupting the people of Europe in the name of Christianity.

How different it would have been if the Roman church had paid attention to the letter to the Romans! As the church lost its love for and understanding of the Jewish people, God severed it from its roots. Paul predicted this would happen to Christians who become proud, thinking they are superior to the Jews when, in reality, God in His great mercy and kindness grafted them into the natural olive tree of which the Jews were a part:

> Boast not against the branches. But if thou boast, thou bearest not the root, but the root thee. Thou wilt say then, The branches were broken off, that I might be grafted in. Well; because of unbelief they were broken off, and thou standest by faith. Be not highminded, but fear: For if God spared not the natural branches, take heed lest he also spare not thee. Behold therefore the goodness and severity of God: on them which fell, severity; but toward thee, goodness, if thou continue in

his goodness: otherwise thou also shalt be cut off. And they also, if they abide not still in unbelief, shall be grafted in: for God is able to graft them in again. (Romans 11:18-23)

Likewise, in being severed from the olive tree, the church was severed from the fruit of the Holy Spirit—"love, joy, peace, longsuffering, gentleness, goodness, faith, meekness, temperance [self-control]" (Galatians 5:22-23)—but rather the works of the flesh manifested in the cruel and corrupt church of the Middle Ages and beyond.

When I was a student, I remember seeing a film of Bernard Malamud's book, *The Fixer,* which made a great impression on me. In this story, Yakov Bok, a Jew living in Tsarist Russia, is wrongly accused of murder and imprisoned. The case is a typical example of the anti-Semitism rife in Russia at the end of the 19th century. The authorities involve the Russian Orthodox Church in their interrogations of Bok by trying to force him to convert to Christianity. They give him a New Testament to read, which he does. When the Russian Orthodox priest comes to interrogate Yakov to find out what he has learned from the New Testament, he states simply, "Jesus is Jewish. So whoever hates the Jew hates Jesus." This is absolutely true, and hatred for the Jews demonstrates a spirit of force, tyranny, and prejudice, which is the absolute opposite of the true spirit of Jesus, the Messiah. Should you visit a church that bears the fruit of anti-Semitism, just remember that the word *Ichabod* signifies that the glory of the Lord has departed (1 Samuel 4:21).

CHAPTER 3

OUT OF NIGHT

———◆———

During the 1970s, Nikki and I used to go and talk to people involved in left-wing political groups about our faith. We made friends with some Jewish socialists who invited us along to a meeting of Young Mapam, a socialist Zionist group. The speaker was a man called Hyam Maccoby who gave a talk on Jesus as a Jewish revolutionary leader against the Romans. We pitched into the discussion afterwards, and some members of the group then invited us along to another meeting where they were going to read pieces of literature which meant something to them.

One of the readings was from a book by Elie Wiesel called *Night* about his experiences in Auschwitz. After the reading, someone asked us, "Where was God when the six million were killed?" I really did not know what to say, and so I went away to read *Night* for myself and think through the issues involved.

My first reaction after reading *Night* was, "How can I who was born when these events were already history, who has no trace of Jewish blood in my veins, presume to write about an experience so terrible, so far removed from my own experience of life and so painful to the Jewish people?" The answer which came to me was clear: "If you have no answer to the questions raised by this book, how can you claim that Jesus is the answer?"

May 1944—Newly arrived Jews from Subcarpathian Rus get off the train in Auschwitz-Birkenau.

February 28, 1941—Dutch Jews wearing prison uniforms marked with a yellow star and the letter "N," for Netherlands, stand at attention during a roll call at the Buchenwald concentration camp (the camp Elie Wiesel was at).

The most eloquent statement of this despair is to be found in *Night* when the author, as a child, views Birkenau, the reception center for Auschwitz, for the first time:

> Flames were leaping from a ditch, gigantic flames. They were burning something. A lorry drew up at the pit and delivered its load—little children. Babies! Yes, I saw it—saw it with my own eyes . . . those little children in the flames. (Is it surprising that I could not sleep after that? Sleep had fled from my eyes).

> Never shall I forget that night, the first night in camp, which has turned my life into one long night, seven times cursed and seven times sealed. . . . Never shall I forget the little faces of the children, whose bodies I saw turned into wreaths of smoke beneath a silent blue sky. Never shall I forget those flames which consumed my faith forever. Never shall I forget that nocturnal silence which deprived me, for all eternity, of the desire to live. Never shall I forget those moments which murdered my God and my soul and turned my dreams to dust. Never shall I forget those things, even if I am condemned to live as long as God Himself. Never. [1]

So where was God? When such appalling evils take place, is it still possible to believe in the concept of a just God, of a God who loves and cares about humanity? Facing this question is more than just an academic exercise. Cruel dictatorships, concentration camps, torture, and utter wickedness still hold sway in many parts of the Earth, and the Bible warns that in the last days evil men will grow worse and worse and that the whole world will ultimately come under the power of the Antichrist of whom Hitler was a major forerunner.

WHO WAS RESPONSIBLE?

The first question which must be asked is, "Who was responsible for creating the death camps and the Nazi terror—God or man?" In *Night*, Elie Wiesel describes the pious Jews in the camp holding services to worship God on Jewish holy days. This caused him to rage against God for allowing these death camps to exist. (As a point of information, the view expressed here represents Elie Wiesel's reaction as a child to the horrors he was witnessing. Later as an adult, he maintained his belief in God.*):

> Thousands of voices repeated the benediction; thousands of men prostrated themselves like trees before a tempest.
>
> Blessed be the name of the Eternal!
>
> Why, but why should I bless Him? In every fiber I rebelled. Because He had thousands of children burned in His pits? Because He kept six crematories working night and day, on Sundays and feast days? Because in His great might He had created Auschwitz, Birkenau, Buna, and so many factories of death?[2]

This is a very understandable reaction to the enormous suffering of the camps. God is supposed to be in control of the universe; one finds oneself the victim of unbelievable wickedness and cruelty. God appears to be doing nothing about it; therefore, God must be responsible for the evil or just indifferent and powerless.

However, God did not create Auschwitz or any factories of death. People did, people who were motivated by Nazism, an ideology which expressed in its ideas and practice a rebellion against God on a hitherto unknown scale in human history. God did not create Auschwitz; He created human beings perfect, to live in peace and harmony with God and each other. However, since the Fall (Genesis 3), sin has reigned over the human race, and the hostile power of Satan has influenced humanity to rebel against God and disobey His commandments. We have come a long way from Cain taking Abel into the field to murder him to the concentration camps and the frightful weapons of destruction of our time. Nevertheless, the principle remains the

---

* Elie Wiesel passed away on July 2, 2016 at the age of 87.

same, and the problem remains the same—sin in the heart of human beings. As the Bible says:

> The heart is deceitful above all things, and desperately wicked: who can know it? (Jeremiah 17:9)

> For from within, out of the heart of men, proceed evil thoughts, adulteries, fornications, murders, thefts, covetousness, wickedness, deceit, lasciviousness, an evil eye, blasphemy, pride, foolishness: All these evil things come from within, and defile the man. (Mark 7:21-23)

> For we have before proved both Jews and Gentiles, that they are all under sin; As it is written, There is none righteous, no, not one: There is none that understandeth, there is none that seeketh after God. They are all gone out of the way, they are together become unprofitable; there is none that doeth good, no, not one. . . . Their feet are swift to shed blood: Destruction and misery are in their ways: And the way of peace have they not known. (Romans 3:9-12, 15-17)

Twentieth-century history testifies absolutely to this analysis of the human condition. It is significant that such an extreme manifestation of the evil in the human heart took place in a century which began with many people putting their trust in the innate goodness of humanity, the perfectibility of human nature, and the coming of a Golden Age of peace, prosperity, and tolerance through advances in science, education, and politics. What is more, it took place in a country whose contribution to European culture was enormous and which had produced some of the leading 19th century writers and philosophers, many of whom rejected God and placed their trust in man's ability to save himself through his own efforts. If anything, the Nazi Holocaust should make us lose faith in this kind of optimistic humanism rather than the God of the Bible. This is the implication of the foreword to *Night* in which the French writer, Francois Mauriac writes about trainloads of Jewish children he saw being taken away from Paris during the Nazi occupation:

> The dream which western man conceived in the 18th century, whose dawn he thought he saw in 1789 [the French Revolution], and which until August 2nd 1914 [the outbreak of the first world war], had grown stronger with the progress of enlightenment and the discoveries of science—this dream finally vanished from me before those trainloads of little children.[3]

THE NAZIS AND GOD

Those who blame God for the Nazi Holocaust should note that the roots of the Nazi ideology lay in a definite rejection, indeed a bitter hatred of not just Judaism, but the God of the Bible and authentic Christianity. In this connection, it is interesting to note the following thoughts written by Friedrich Nietzsche, the German philosopher who first proclaimed that "God is dead."

> That the strong races of Northern Europe have not repudiated the Christian God certainly reflects no credit on their talent for religion.[4]

> [Speaking of the Christian concept of God] [T]he God of the "great majority," the democrat among Gods [N.B. Nietzsche loathed democracy], has none the less not become a proud pagan God . . . he has remained the god of the nook, the God of all dark corners and places, of all the unhealthy quarters throughout the world![5]

> What is good?—All that heightens the feeling of power, the will to power, power itself in man. What is bad?—All that proceeds from weakness. What is happiness?—The feeling that power *increases*—that resistance is overcome. *Not* contentment, but more power; *not* peace at all, but war; *not*

virtue, but proficiency. . . . The weak and ill-constituted shall perish: first principle of *our* philanthropy. And one shall help them to do so. What is more harmful than any vice?—Active sympathy for the weak and ill-constituted: Christianity.[6]

Christianity is called the religion of pity.—Pity stands in the antithesis to the tonic emotions which enhance the energy of the feeling of life: it has a depressive effect. . . . Pity on the whole thwarts the law of evolution, which is the law of *selection*. It preserves what is ripe for destruction; it defends life's disinherited and condemned.[7]

THOSE WHO BLAME GOD FOR THE

NAZI HOLOCAUST SHOULD NOTE THAT

THE ROOTS OF THE NAZI IDEOLOGY

LAY IN A DEFINITE REJECTION, INDEED

A BITTER HATRED OF NOT JUST

JUDAISM, BUT THE GOD OF THE BIBLE

AND AUTHENTIC CHRISTIANITY

This philosophy of 19th century German atheism clearly has a spiritual link to Nazi ideology. One wonders what Nietzsche would have thought of the strong, powerful, pitiless ones, the SS, "selecting" the fittest specimens as they ran past them naked—the strong to be worked to death in concentration camps, the weak and "ill-constituted" to be taken away to the gas chambers. What does the modern world need, hard, pitiless anti-Christian men and women, or those who will follow the One that Nietzsche despises so much who said?:

Blessed are the poor in spirit: for theirs is the kingdom of heaven. . . . Blessed are the meek: for they shall inherit the earth. . . . Blessed are the merciful: for they shall obtain mercy. . . . Blessed are the peacemakers: for they shall be called the children of God. (Matthew 5:3, 5, 7, 9)

There is no doubt what kind of people Hitler wanted. He said "Antiquity was better than modern times because it did not know Christianity and syphilis." His main reasons for rejecting Christianity were as follows:

1. It was a religion that sided with everything weak and low.

2. It was purely Jewish and Oriental in origin. Christians "bend their backs to the sound of church bells and crawl to the cross of a foreign God."

3. The religion began 2000 years ago among sick, exhausted, and despairing men who had lost their belief in life.

4. Christian ideas of "forgiveness of sin," "resurrection," and "salvation" were just nonsense.

5. The Christian idea of mercy was dangerous. One must never extend mercy to his enemies. "Mercy is an un-German conception."

6. Christian "love" was silly; love paralyzes.

7. The Christian idea of equality of all human beings meant that the inferior, the ill, the crippled, the criminal, and the weak were protected.[8]

The Nazis may have marched into battle with "Gott mit uns" (God with us) as their motto, but their god was a pagan antichrist god, and they followed a false messiah, Adolf Hitler, and bowed down before idols of power, physical force, and the dream of world domination by the *Teutonic Master Race*. Is it surprising that the fruit of this demonic ideology was the nightmare of destruction and slaughter which followed in their wake?

They may also have professed some *sort* of Christianity, but their aim was to replace authentic Christianity with a program for a "new" Christianity, which consisted of:

- Throw out the Old Testament—it is a Jewish book. Also throw out parts of the New Testament.

- Christ must be regarded not as Jewish, but as a Nordic martyr put to death by the Jews, a kind of warrior who by His death saved the world from Jewish domination.

- Adolph Hitler is the new Messiah sent to earth to rescue the world from the Jews.

- The swastika succeeds the cross as the symbol of German Christianity.

- German land, German blood, German soul, German art—these four must become the most sacred things of all to the German Christian.[9]

In effect, the Nazis were replacing Christianity with a new paganism which drew its strength from Wagner's music and the Nordic myths of pre-Christian times. One of the prime movers in this direction was Alfred Rosenburg to whom Hitler awarded the National Prize, Germany's version of the Nobel Prize, in 1937. Rosenburg wanted a return to the old Teutonic religion of fire and sword. There was even a hymn for the new German Faith Movement:

The time of the Cross has gone now,
The Sunwheel shall arise,
And so, with God, we shall be free at last
And give our people their honor back.[10]

SO WHERE *WAS* GOD?

A Jewish novel, *The Last of the Just* by André Schwartz-Bart, traces Jewish suffering through many generations and concludes in the time of the Holocaust. There is a very moving scene when a crowd of worshipping Jews leaves a synagogue and is confronted by Nazi troops in the courtyard:

> Ernie had a staggering intuition—that God was hovering above the synagogue courtyard, vigilant and ready to intervene. . . . Ernie felt that God was there, so close that with a little boldness he might have touched him. "Stop! Don't touch my people!" he murmured as if the divine voice had found expression in his own frail throat.[11]

In the novel, there is a momentary deliverance on that occasion; however, the terrible cycle of death and destruction brought about by the Nazis continued with the massacre of six million Jews and the deaths of millions of Gentiles on the battlefronts and in the concentration camps. Was God silent and indifferent while all this was going on?

God was neither silent nor indifferent, but He was watching and weeping over the wickedness of humanity and the suffering of the people, especially the Jewish people. However, because He has given us free will, the consequence of the wrong choice made by the German people was played out in the events which followed. The final defeat of the Nazis showed God's ultimate judgment on that wicked political system.

While God was not silent or indifferent, unfortunately much of the church was. There were indeed brave souls, like the ten Boom family in Holland who sacrificed themselves to rescue Jews from the Nazis. But for the most part, the church failed to speak out, and not surprisingly many Jewish people saw "Christians" as the enemy. In the novel *The Last of the Just,* Ernie Levy, the lead character, marries Golda the night before they are to be taken away to a concentration camp. Their conversation turns to Jesus:

"Oh Ernie," Golda said, "you know them. Tell me why do the Christians hate us the way they do? They seem so nice when I can look at them without my star.

Ernie put his arm round her shoulder solemnly. "It's very mysterious," he murmured in Yiddish. "They don't exactly know why themselves. I've been in their churches and I've read their gospel. Do you know who the Christ was? A simple Jew like your father. A kind of Hassid.

Golda smiled gently. "You're kidding me."

No, no believe me, and I'll bet they'd have got along fine, the two of them, because he was really a good Jew, you know sort of like the Baal Shem Tov[12]—a merciful man, and gentle. The Christians say they love him, but I think they hate him without knowing it. So they take the cross by the other end and make a sword out of it and strike us with it! You understand Golda," he cried out suddenly strangely excited, "*they take the cross and they turn it around, they turn it around, my God. . . .*[13]

Jesus was much more than "a simple Jew," but the fact that He was a Jew is one which is totally obvious from the New Testament. Those who call themselves Christians and yet hate the Jews need to repent of anti-Semitism and determine to stand by Jewish people when they suffer persecution, recognizing that the root of anti-Semitism is human hostility to God. Rabbi David Panitz has pointed out in this connection that "the need for atonement through admission of the facts of history is an established Hebraic and Christian doctrine. Until you admit you have been wrong, you cannot begin a reconstruction of your life."

The professing Christian church has an enormous burden of guilt in relation to the Jewish people. Although Nazi philosophy was pagan and anti-Christian, the seeds of anti-Semitism reaped by the Nazis were sown by the churches in their denunciations of the

Jews. At the same time, we have to say that the real Jesus is entirely different from the cruel caricature who takes the cross to beat the Jewish people with. In Ernie Levy's conversation with Golda, he goes on to say:

> Poor Jesus, if he came back to the earth and saw that the pagans had made a sword out of him and used it against his sisters and brothers, he'd be sad, he'd grieve forever. And maybe he does see it.[14]

CHAPTER 4

SO WHAT ABOUT
THE MESSIAH?

◆

T he sufferings of the Jewish people have led many to disbelieve in God and to reject the idea of the Messiah altogether. But for others, the expectation of the Messiah coming is a hope that times of pain and persecution will end and peace will come to the house of Israel. A Jewish prayer says:

> Thou, O God hast promised to redeem us: hasten therefore the period of our redemption . . . The enemy wounds our heart, throws stones at us, afflicts us, treads us underfoot, and scoffs both at us and our hope of redemption. . . . But the daughter of Zion may indeed rejoice for our Messiah cometh.[1]

The big question is "How do we identify the Messiah?" These are some answers I have heard from Jewish people:

- Messiah is a great man who will create world peace, rebuild the Temple in Jerusalem, and bring the Jewish people back to the Torah.

- Messiah is the Lubavitcher Rebbe, Rabbi Menachem Schneerson, who died in 1994 and who will rise again from the dead.[2]

- There is no personal Messiah, but there will be a Messianic age in which people will live in peace and harmony together and wars will cease.

- There is no Messiah and the whole idea is a superstition, which Jewish people need to put behind them so they can work out their problems by themselves.

The first of these options is the most Orthodox view. According to Moses Maimonides, who lived from 1135 to 1204 and whose writings, especially *Guide to the Perplexed*, are a major influence on modern Judaism, the sign of the Messiah is as follows:

> In future time, the King Messiah will arise and renew the Davidic dynasty, restoring it to its initial sovereignty. He will rebuild the Beit Ha Mikdash [Temple] and gather in the dispersed remnant of Israel. Then in his days all the statutes will be reinstated as in former times. We will offer sacrifices and observe the Sabbath and Jubilee years according to all their particulars set forth in the Torah. . . .

> If a king will arise from the House of David who delves deeply into the study of the Torah and, like David his ancestor, observes its mitzvoth [commandments] as prescribed by the Written Law and the Oral Law; if he will compel all of Israel to walk in the way of the Torah and repair the breaches in its observance; and if he will fight the wars of God; we may with assurance consider him Messiah.

> If he succeeds in the above, builds the Beit Ha Mikdash on its site, and gathers in the dispersed remnant of Israel, he is definitely the Messiah.[3]

Following this, it is said he will bring about a perfect world:

He will then perfect the entire world, motivating all the nations to serve God together, as it is written, I will make the peoples pure of speech so that they will all call upon the Name of God and serve him with one purpose.[4]

From this, we deduce that the Messiah has to show He is Messiah by completing the following three tasks:

1. Regather the dispersed Jewish people to Israel.

2. Rebuild the Temple in Jerusalem.

3. Make world peace.

By contrast, it is pointed out that since the coming of Jesus, the following has happened:

1. The Jewish people were dispersed into the nations.

2. The Temple in Jerusalem was destroyed.

3. There have been wars and persecutions ever since.

Maimonides said about Christianity:

Can there be a greater stumbling block than Christianity? All the prophets spoke of Messiah as the redeemer of Israel and their Saviour, who would gather their dispersed ones and strengthen their observance of the mitzvoth. In contrast the founder of Christianity caused the Jews to be slain by the sword, their remnants to be scattered and humiliated, the Torah to be altered, and the majority of the world to err and serve a god other than the Lord.[5]

Therefore, Jesus is not the Messiah. End of argument.

Except that it is not the end of the argument. The argument has raged for centuries, and I do not expect this book to be the last word on it! The book, which is the last word on the subject of the Messiah, the Bible, is the one we need to turn to. Sadly, this is a book which is on many people's bookshelves, but not very much in their hearts and minds. It may be the world's bestseller, but it is not the world's best-read book. Even those who read it, Jewish and Christian, often try to explain it away, reducing it to the realm of myth and therefore an unsure guide to anything, particularly the identity of the Messiah (if there is one!). On the subject of the Messiah, the writer of the "Ask the Rabbi" column in the *Jewish Chronicle* denied that details of Messiah's coming could be found by searching the Hebrew prophets, an approach which he said "biblical criticism has rendered hopelessly out of date."[6]

I believe the day will come when *biblical criticism* will be rendered hopelessly out of date as people wake up to the fact that the prophecies of the Bible have astonishing relevance to what is happening today.

I began to take the Bible seriously at the age of 23 after wandering through a variety of alternative worldviews, including Marxism, during the 1960s. What made me begin to look into its ancient pages for the direction of my life was the realization that it is not just a dusty old book with some nice stories in it but rather a living word which speaks into the world situation today and into our individual lives.

On the subject of Israel, the Bible speaks of the scattering of the Jewish people into the nations and their return to the land of Israel at the end of days, with a time of trouble taking place, centering on Jerusalem while involving all the nations of Earth (Jeremiah 30-31, Ezekiel 36-39, Zechariah 12-14).

Israel scattered and regathered is to be a sign of God's purposes and faithfulness:

> Hear the word of the LORD, O ye nations, and declare it in the isles afar off, and say, He that scattered Israel will gather him, and keep him, as a shepherd doth his flock. (Jeremiah 31:10)

Ezekiel 36 speaks of the land of Israel becoming desolate as the Jewish people are driven from it and Gentiles possess it. But then it becomes a fertile land again with trees being planted on its hills and its ancient cities rebuilt when the Jewish people return. God says:

> For I will take you from among the heathen, and gather you out of all countries, and will bring you into your own land. (Ezekiel 36: 24)

At such a time, the nations round about will oppose Israel and by "crafty counsel" (i.e. deception; Psalm 83:3) make a confederacy with the aim of driving Israel into the sea. They will say:

> Come, and let us cut them off from being a nation; that the name of Israel may be no more in remembrance. (Psalm 83:4)

The conflict over the land of Israel and especially over the city of Jerusalem will involve all the nations of the world in the last days of this age.

> And in that day will I make Jerusalem a burdensome stone for all people: all that burden themselves with it shall be cut in pieces, though all the people of the earth be gathered together against it. (Zechariah 12:3)

Today, all nations, in the form of the United Nations, are trying in vain to solve the question of who should rule Jerusalem. These prophecies coming to pass in our time are a sure sign of the faithfulness of God to His Word and of the coming of the Messiah to sort out the mess human beings have made of the world God gave us to look after.

There are many other signs in current events which point us to the conclusion that we are living in the last days of this age, when God will intervene to rescue the world from absolute disaster. For example, a collapse of moral values with evil going from nation to nation as in the days of Noah and Sodom and Gomorrah, massive environmental destruction, and lawlessness pushing the nations into a catastrophic world situation from which only God will be able to rescue us. I have written a book, *Countdown to Calamity*, which has details of these things and is available from the address at the end of this book. I also produce a quarterly magazine *Light for the Last Days* which looks at current events in the light of Bible prophecy.

If the writers of the Bible were simply putting down their *own* thoughts for their *own* generation, then their words are interesting but not reliable as a guide to the perplexed people of the 21st century, whether Jewish or Gentile. But if they wrote under the inspiration of the Holy Spirit as God showed them things to come, then it is utter folly to ignore their words and their message for today.

We must therefore turn our attention to the writers of the Hebrew Bible in our search for truth about the identity of the Messiah. Here we find that the issue of the Messiah is more complex than the conclusion Maimonides came to in the quotations shown earlier in this chapter. Is he right when he says that "the founder of Christianity (i.e. Jesus) caused the world to err and follow a god other than the Lord"?

Concerning the Messiah and the end of days, the prophecies in the Tenach* appear to be saying contradictory things. For example, the prophet Isaiah alone presents the following difficulties:

- Chapter 2 of the Book of Isaiah speaks of Messiah reigning with power from Jerusalem, with all nations going to hear the word of the Lord and as a result living in peace together.

- Chapter 53 speaks of Messiah being despised and rejected of men, having our iniquities laid on Him, when He is cut off from the land of the living, executed with transgressors, buried, and yet living to see the "travail of his soul." (Much of modern Judaism follows Rashi in denying that Isaiah 53 is about the Messiah, and rather claims that the "servant" refers to Israel. We will look at arguments about this in Chapter 7 of this book.)

- Chapter 11 speaks of the future condition of the Earth in the end of days—when the earth will be full of the knowledge of

---

*Tenach is the Jewish Bible (Old Testament) arranged in a slightly different order from the Christian Bible, but the same in content.

the Lord as the waters cover the sea, returning to conditions of paradise, with even the animals being vegetarian and not devouring each other.

• Chapter 24 speaks of the future condition also associated with the end of days in which the earth is devastated, cities are destroyed, and people scorched with few survivors.

These paradoxes are reflected in the ways in which Orthodox Judaism interprets the signs of the coming Messiah. A leaflet I was given on the street by members of the Lubavitch movement spreading their faith says we are living in the days leading up to the coming of the Messiah:

All the signs indicate that we are nearing the end of days . . . It is certain beyond a shadow of doubt that the era of redemption has arrived . . . All that is required is to greet our righteous Moshiach [Messiah], so that he can fulfil his mission and redeem all Israel from exile.[7]

In the early 1990s, members of Lubavitch, under the inspiration of their Rebbe, began demanding that God send the Messiah under the slogan "We want Moshiach now." They presented an optimistic view of the end of days, seeing such events as the fall of Communism and Israel's protection during the first Gulf War as signs that redemption is near:

We are living in the most extraordinary times as our world evolves towards a state of peace, and mankind thrives towards a state of perfection. The times are changing not just for the better but for the best. A cornerstone of Jewish faith is the belief that ultimately good and peace must triumph. This is the essence of Moshiach who will usher in the final redemption ordained in the Torah.[8]

On the other hand, in his book *Prophecy and Providence,* Rabbi Sokolovsky argues that the era of "Ikveta d'Meshicha" (the heels of Messiah—i.e., the last days of this age) will be days of spiritual decline and trouble. This is illustrated by the following quotations from the Talmud:

> Tragedy will come upon you at the end of all the days.[9] (Targum Yonathan)

> During the era preceding the Moshiach, prices will soar. The vine will produce its fruit but wine will be very expensive.[10] (Sotah 49b)

> During the Ikveta d'Meshicha (the era preceding the Messiah) insolence will abound.. The young will make the faces of the elderly grow ashen with shame; the elderly will have to rise before the young; sons will disgrace fathers; daughters will rise up against their mothers; the members of one's family will become his enemies.[11] (Sotah 49b)

> During the Ikveta d'Meshicha government will turn atheist and there will be no protest. Truth will vanish.[12] (Sanhedrin 97a, Sotah 49b)

The Talmud recognizes that the Messianic prophecies are not straight forward and that alternative possibilities exist concerning the coming of the Messiah. He may come on the clouds of Heaven in triumph as a reigning king or riding on a donkey in humility. The way he comes depends on the spiritual state of the generation he comes to. He may come in glory to a spiritual generation, or in humility to an unspiritual generation.[13]

Another explanation for the problem of the different portraits of the Messiah is the idea that two Messiahs are coming. The first one to suffer and die is called Moshiach ben Yoseph (Messiah, son of Joseph), meaning he will be like Joseph in his sufferings and rejected by his brethren. The second one will rule and reign and is called Moshiach ben David (Messiah, son of David), meaning he will rule in triumph like King David.[14] Modern Judaism has largely forgotten this line of interpretation and written Messiah, son of Joseph, out of the script, but this concept of two Messiahs coming with different missions and experience is a recognized rabbinic response to the problems posed by the text of the Bible.

An alternative way to resolve this question is the view that there are two comings of the same Messiah. First, He comes as a Suffering Servant (Isaiah 53), coming in humility on the back of a donkey, as Jesus did when He rode into Jerusalem in fulfillment of Zechariah's prophecy at the beginning of the final week leading to His sacrificial death and resurrection. The second time He will come on the clouds of Heaven as Jesus told the Sanhedrin He would at His trial:

Art thou the Christ [the Messiah], the Son of the Blessed?

And Jesus said, I am: and ye shall see the Son of man sitting on the right hand of power, and coming in the clouds of heaven. (Mark 14:61-62)

We will look at this subject in more detail in chapter 10 of this book, but before we do, let us look at some major objections in Judaism to Jesus' claim to be the Messiah.

And there shall come forth a rod out of the stem of Jesse, and a
Branch shall grow out of his roots: and the spirit of the LORD
shall rest upon him, the spirit of wisdom and understanding,
the spirit of counsel and might, the spirit of knowledge
and of the fear of the LORD; and shall make him of quick
understanding in the fear of the LORD: and he shall not judge
after the sight of his eyes, neither reprove after the hearing of his
ears: but with righteousness shall he judge the poor, and reprove
with equity for the meek of the earth: and he shall smite the
earth with the rod of his mouth, and with the breath of his lips
shall he slay the wicked. And righteousness shall be the girdle of
his loins, and faithfulness the girdle of his reins. (Isaiah 11:1-5)

CHAPTER 5

MESSIAH—A GREAT MAN OR A DIVINE PERSON?

———————◆———————

By far, the biggest stumbling block to any consideration of Jesus being the Messiah is the Christian claim that He is equal with God. I was discussing this question with an Orthodox Jewish friend. He said that such an idea is completely impossible for Jewish people to accept. So I asked him, "What is your idea of the Messiah?"

He said that the Messiah is a great man, not a divine person, who brings peace to the world.

I responded that for any man to bring peace to the world is an enormous task beyond the ability of any mere human. And besides, there is one logical problem. If he is just a great man, what happens when he dies?

His answer was that the Messiah will set up a way of life, a new system, which people will fit into because of his teaching. I said that the problem with human beings is that they don't fit into systems.

In his book *The Real Messiah?*, which attempts to refute the view that Jesus is Messiah, Rabbi Kaplan puts it like this:

> The Jewish concept of the Messiah is that which is clearly developed by the prophets of the Bible. He is a leader of the Jews, strong in wisdom, power and spirit. It is he who will bring complete redemption to the Jewish people, both spiritually

and physically. Along with this he will bring eternal peace, love, prosperity, and moral perfection to the entire world. The Jewish Messiah is truly human in origin. He is born of ordinary human parents, and is of flesh and blood like all mortals.[1]

So a *mortal* is going to bring *eternal* peace and perfection? The essence of being mortal is that one is going to die someday.

In the early 1990s, some members of the Lubavitch movement began to believe that their leader, Rabbi Menachem Schneerson, was the King Messiah. Then he had a stroke and later died. Unable to cope with the idea that the old man in his nineties had come to the end of his natural life, supporters of the Messianic tendency in Lubavitch began to believe he would rise from the dead! If he is more than just an old man dying and really is the Messiah, then there is a certain logic in believing he will rise from the dead. If not, this view is farfetched to say the least!

This belief has been pronounced heretical by mainstream Judaism and for a rather obvious reason. Rabbi David Berger wrote:

> There is no possibility whatsoever that the Rebbe would emerge from the dead to be the Messiah. That could be possible in the Christian faith but not in Judaism. The very suggestion is repugnant to everything Judaism represents.[2]

We would agree there is no possibility that the Rebbe could emerge from the dead to be the Messiah. However, the real Messiah does need to have power over death if He is to deal permanently with the problems which afflict the human race. In fact, He has to have an endless life and to be an eternal person Himself. He has got to be on hand all the time, for all the people of the world to deal with their problems. All of which makes Him anything but a normal man born of ordinary human parents of flesh and blood.

The Tenach indicates that the Messiah will be more than a normal man. A number of Scriptures point to His supernatural origin, even to His divine nature. In the prophecy of Micah 5:2, we read of one who is to be "Ruler in Israel":

> But thou, Bethlehem Ephratah, though thou be little among the thousands of Judah, yet out of thee shall he come forth unto me that is to be ruler in Israel; whose goings forth have been from of old, from everlasting.

THE REAL MESSIAH NEEDS TO HAVE POWER OVER DEATH IF HE IS TO DEAL PERMANENTLY WITH THE PROBLEMS WHICH AFFLICT THE HUMAN RACE. IN FACT, HE HAS TO HAVE AN ENDLESS LIFE AND TO BE AN ETERNAL PERSON HIMSELF.

The one who is to come out of Bethlehem in Judea will have an origin which is "from everlasting" (*mimei olam*—literally from the days of eternity). Whose origins are from the days of eternity? Only God. Therefore, this prophecy points to someone who will not just be a "Ruler in Israel" (i.e. a king or governor) but the Messiah. He will come forth from Bethlehem as far as His earthly existence is concerned, but His real origin will be in eternity.

In Isaiah 9, we read of one who is to be born a child and yet who is the Mighty God (*el gibbor*) and the Everlasting Father (*avi ad*):

> For unto us a child is born, unto us a son is given: and the government shall be upon his shoulder: and his name shall be called Wonderful, Counsellor, The mighty God, The everlasting Father, The Prince of Peace. Of the increase of

his government and peace there shall be no end, upon the throne of David, and upon his kingdom, to order it, and to establish it with judgment and with justice from henceforth even for ever. The zeal of the LORD of hosts will perform this. (Isaiah 9:6-7)

How can someone be a son and the Everlasting Father at the same time? If he is a mortal reigning on David's throne, how can he establish it with judgment and justice forever? Why is he called "the Mighty God"? One rabbinic explanation of these verses is that they refer to the godly King Hezekiah, but this does not make sense. The one spoken of being born as a male child has to be at the same time an eternal person. In fact, He has to be God.

In Jeremiah 23:5, we read of the descendant of David who is clearly identified as the King Messiah. In the next verse, we read:

In his days Judah shall be saved, and Israel shall dwell safely: and this is his name whereby he shall be called, THE LORD OUR RIGHTEOUSNESS. (Jeremiah 23:6)

The name given to the Messiah contains the divine name, a clear indication that the Messiah is to be a divine being.

But how can the Messiah be a divine person if there is one God who is indivisible and rules in Heaven? Can God leave ruling the universe to come to Earth? Did God ever appear in human form in the Tenach?

I heard a cassette of an interview given in the USA with a Jewish lady named Sharon Allen. Sharon had been raised in a very Orthodox Jewish home. Her marriage to an Orthodox Jew in New York had failed, and she moved with her daughter to the west coast of America. There she married a Gentile businessman who loved Jewish ways and actually helped to build a new synagogue which they attended as a family together. After a while, Sharon said to her husband, "You're so Jewish. Why don't you convert to Judaism?" He agreed and was told there were three things he had to do.

1. Be circumcised. No problem, he had been circumcised as a baby.

2. Be immersed in water in the mikveh (ritual bath) to show his identification with the Jewish people. No problem.

3. Appear before the Beth Din (religious court) and formally renounce whatever or whoever he had believed in before. Problem.

To Sharon's amazement, he said he could not renounce Jesus. As he had never been a vocal Christian or attended church during their marriage, this came as a shock to her. But then she thought, "No problem. Everything that God wants us to know about the Messiah is in the Jewish Bible. I'll read the Bible and prove to my husband that Jesus cannot be the Messiah."

She then prayed to God to show her the truth about the Messiah and began reading the Jewish Bible in Hebrew (in which she was fluent) from beginning to end. She never opened the New Testament, but as she read the Tenach, she could not believe what she was reading and the conclusion she was coming to. Everywhere she found references to Jesus. The miracles He did, the death He would die, the fact He would be received by the Gentiles.

Apart from the prophecies which speak about the Messiah, she could not come to terms with the person described in the Bible as the Angel of the Lord, Malach Adonai, who appeared at various times to people in the Bible. They react to Him as though they are seeing God. They are afraid they are going to die as a result. He gives the Word of God; He has the power to forgive sins. Who is He?

She began to read commentaries—the Artscroll series, Rashi's commentary, and whatever she could find to give answers to her questions. The uncomfortable conclusion she was coming to was that far from proving Jesus was not the Messiah, the Hebrew Bible was giving her reasons to believe He was. Finding no convincing answer, she spoke to her rabbi who put her on to the leading anti-missionary rabbis in the USA. Finally, she went to a lecture by Rabbi Immanuel Shochet at her daughter's school on why Jewish people should not believe in Jesus.

The Rabbi said that no Jewish person who had been raised in a kosher Jewish home and kept all the traditions could believe in "that man" (Jesus). During the question time after his talk, Sharon raised her hand and told him she had been raised in a kosher Jewish home and kept all the traditions, but the more she studied the Jewish Bible the more she came to see that Jesus fitted with the Jewish expectation of the Messiah.

The major theological problem she presented to the rabbi was the question of the appearances of the Lord in the Jewish Bible. The logical conclusion she was coming to was, "If God can appear in human form to the Patriarchs, why is it considered impossible for God to appear in human form in the person of the Messiah?" If this is so, then one of Judaism's major theological objections to Jesus being the Messiah is removed. The rabbi, considered the expert in the field of refuting the claim that Jesus is Messiah, could not answer her questions to her satisfaction, and so she decided to read the New Testament for herself. At this point, all her objections were swept away, and she came to the conclusion that Jesus is the Messiah.[3]

So does the Jewish Bible point to God being a plural unity, which is vital to the view that Jesus is the Messiah, or does it describe God as an absolute indivisible unity, which is vital to the view that He is not? Did God appear in human form in the Jewish Bible?

In the very first verse of the Bible, we read, "In the beginning God created the heaven and the earth" (Genesis 1:1). The word for "God" (Elohim) is a masculine plural noun. The word for "created" (*bara*) is a singular verb. The very first sentence of the Bible, with a plural noun and a singular verb, opens up the possibility of God being a plural unity. In Genesis 1:26, God said, "Let us make man in our image, after our likeness." Why not, "Let me make man in my image"? It cannot be that God is speaking to the angels because man is not made in the image of angels. The rabbinic explanation, that majesty is addressed in the plural, does not add up either since there is no example in the Bible of kings addressing themselves in the plural. The likely explanation for this and other occasions where

God speaks in the plural of Himself (Genesis 11:7, Isaiah 6:8) is that God is a plural unity.

The Bible, especially the Torah, has examples of a physical manifestation of God appearing to people. In Genesis 3:8, we read that Adam and Eve "heard the voice of the LORD God walking in the garden in the cool of the day: and Adam and his wife hid themselves from the presence of the LORD God amongst the trees of the garden." This shows a physical presence, someone walking in the garden from whom Adam and Eve thought they could hide.

In Genesis 18:1, we read, "And the LORD appeared unto him [Abraham] in the plains of Mamre." Then the text records there were three men before Abraham to whom he gave food. Interestingly, he breaks the rabbinical kosher food laws (but not the Levitical ones) by mixing milk and meat[4]:

> And he took butter, and milk, and the calf which he had dressed, and set it before them; and he stood by them under the tree, and they did eat. (Genesis 18:8)

The Lord then tells Abraham he is going to have a child by Sarah (Genesis 18:9-15). Then the "men" depart for Sodom. Although the text does not tell us that *two* men depart, when we get to chapter 19 verse 1, the text does tell us that two angels (i.e. the men who departed in Genesis 18:16) arrived in Sodom. After the "men" (angels) have departed in verse 16, the Lord then tells Abraham what He is going to do in the coming destruction of Sodom (Genesis 18:17-32). After the Lord has listened to Abraham's plea for mercy for Sodom, the text reads:

> And the LORD went his way, as soon as he had left communing with Abraham: and Abraham returned unto his place. (Genesis 18:33)

The implication of all this is that the three "men" Abraham sees at the beginning of chapter 18 are comprised of two angels who go

Abraham with the three visitors

on to Sodom half way through the chapter and the Lord who stays to the end of the chapter after the two angels have left. So the Lord appears along with the two angels in physical form as a man and eats food with Abraham.

In Genesis 32, Jacob has an encounter as he is about to cross over into the Promised Land, returning with his wives and flocks after twenty years of hard labor for Laban the Syrian. He prays to God, terrified that his brother Esau will get his revenge and kill him for taking his birthright and his father's blessing (Genesis 27). To appease Esau, he sends him gifts and divides his family and flocks into companies in the hope this might give them some protection from being attacked. Having done this, Jacob is alone when the encounter happens:

> And Jacob was left alone; and there wrestled a man with him until the breaking of the day. And when he saw that he prevailed not against him, he touched the hollow of his thigh; and the hollow of Jacob's thigh was out of joint, as he wrestled with him. (Genesis 32:24-25)

To prove this was not just a figment of his imagination Jacob then walked with a permanent limp (Genesis 32:31).

You can't get much more physical than an all-night wrestling match. The person you are wrestling with obviously must have a body. So who was this mysterious man? The next few verses point to the answer:

> And he [the man] said, Let me go, for the day breaketh.

> And he [Jacob] said, I will not let thee go, except thou bless me.

> And he said unto him, What is thy name?

> And he said, Jacob.

> And he said, Thy name shall be called no more Jacob, but
> Israel [means "prince with God"] : for as a prince hast thou
> power with God and with men, and hast prevailed.
>
> And Jacob asked him, and said, Tell me, I pray thee, thy name.
>
> And he said, Wherefore is it that thou dost ask after my name?
> And he blessed him there.
>
> And Jacob called the name of the place Peniel [means "face
> of God"]: for I have seen God face to face, and my life is
> preserved. (Genesis 32:26-30)

The only conclusion one can come to from these verses is that
Jacob identified the man he had wrestled with as being God.

So from these verses, we see that humans had contact with a
being who appeared in human form, but whom they identified as
God. He walked in a garden, He ate food, and He wrestled, all very
physical activities.

At the end of his life, as he was blessing Joseph together with
Joseph's sons, Jacob looked back on the supernatural encounters of
his life and identified these with the "Angel" who had kept him:

> And he [Jacob] blessed Joseph, and said, God, before whom
> my fathers Abraham and Isaac did walk, the God which fed
> me all my life long unto this day, the Angel which redeemed
> me from all evil, bless the lads. (Genesis 48:15-16)

In these verses, he is equating this Angel with God—the one
who has redeemed him and the one he is asking to bless Joseph and
his grandsons.

Then in Exodus 14, we read of the Angel of the Lord (Malach
Adonai), who would go before the Israelites to bring them into the
Promised Land and to fight against their enemies. Concerning this
Angel, the Lord says:

Beware of him, and obey his voice, provoke him not; for he will not pardon your transgressions: for my name is in him. (Exodus 23:21)

This sounds like the authority of God is delegated to Him, and His words are as God's words. He has God's name in Him, and the name implies His nature. He also has power to pardon or not pardon transgressions, something which only God can do.

In the Book of Judges, the Angel of the Lord appears to Manoah and his wife telling them they will bear a son who is to be a Nazirite (one dedicated to God). (This son will be Samson). They ask the angel his name, and He replies, "Why askest thou thus after my name, seeing it is secret?" (Judges 13:18). The Hebrew word for secret used here is *peli,* which is always associated with the wonders of God. Then, when they offer a burnt offering to the Lord, the Angel of the Lord ascends to Heaven in the flame of the altar. Manoah's response to this is to say to his wife, "We shall surely die, because we have seen God" (Judges 13:22). In other words, they recognize that the Angel of the Lord is equal with God.

A major Messianic prophecy is Zechariah 14 which speaks of the Lord coming to rescue Israel from the nations that gather against Jerusalem in the last days of this age. The text says:

Then shall the LORD go forth, and fight against those nations, as when he fought in the day of battle. And his feet shall stand in that day upon the mount of Olives, which is before Jerusalem on the east. (Zechariah 14:3-4)

The word used for the Lord is again the Hebrew name for God. This passage is believed by Orthodox Jews to be about the Messiah coming at the end of days, and today the Mount of Olives is covered in gravestones. It is the most prestigious place to be buried because it is believed that the Messiah will come to the Mount of Olives, blow the trumpet for the resurrection of the dead, and those who are buried there will be the first to be resurrected. The theological problem this raises for Orthodox Jews is that if we agree that Zechariah 14 is about the Messiah (and we do!), then the Messiah is called God. Not only this, but He will also apparently have feet and stand on the Mount of Olives. If He has feet, presumably He will have the rest of a body as well!

We also read of one who is identified as the Son of God in the Jewish Bible. In Psalm 2, which is a parallel passage to Zechariah 14, we read of the Lord dealing with the nations in turmoil and rebellion against Him. In response, God says:

> Yet have I set my king upon my holy hill of Zion. (Psalm 2:6)

He goes on to say of this one:

> Thou art my Son; this day have I begotten thee. Ask of me, and I shall give thee the heathen for thine inheritance, and the uttermost parts of the earth for thy possession. (Psalm 2:7-8)

In Proverbs 30:4, there are a series of questions:

> Who hath ascended up into heaven, or descended? who hath gathered the wind in his fists? who hath bound the waters in a garment? who hath established all the ends of the earth?

The expected answer to all these questions is God. But Proverbs 30:4 completes the verse with a question:

> [W]hat is his name, and what is his son's name, if thou canst tell?

Good question!

When Nebuchadnezzar has the three Hebrew men cast into the burning fiery furnace for refusing to worship his image, they are supernaturally rescued by one identified as the Son of God:

I see four men loose, walking in the midst of the fire, and they have no hurt; and the form of the fourth is like the Son of God. (Daniel 3:25)

The encounters between God and people in the Jewish Bible referred to here imply that God appeared in some recognizable form to humans. Quite often He appeared as a man. Sometimes He is called the Angel of the Lord, sometimes not. Often, the Hebrew word used in these Scriptures contains the divine name which Judaism considers to be so holy that it cannot even be pronounced. Significant prophecies about the coming Messiah imply He will have a divine nature and be much more than a great man.

But doesn't the basic statement of faith of Judaism, the Shema, rule this out? In Deuteronomy 6:4, we read, "Hear, O Israel: The LORD our God is one LORD." God is one, so He can't be three!

Certainly there can't be three gods, but the Shema does not rule out the possibility that God can be a plural unity or three-in-one. Interestingly, it contains the name of God given three times—twice as the divine name pronounced "Adonai"[5] and once as Eloheinu. Eloheinu is a form of Elohim, the name of God given in Genesis 1:1 with the suffix "-enu" used here as the Hebrew way to say "our God." The basic word, Elohim, however, is the plural word for God.

The word *echad* is used in Deuteronomy 6:4 and means one but can mean one in the sense of a unity of more than one. For example, in Genesis 2:24 we read:

Therefore shall a man leave his father and his mother, and shall cleave unto his wife: and they shall be one flesh.

The Hebrew for one flesh is *basar echad*. They become one (echad) through sexual union, but they remain two people. In Judges 20:1, we read of Israel gathering together as "one man" (*ish echad*) before the Lord. They are united as one people, but they are also many individual people.

There is another word for one—*yachid*, which is used in Genesis 22:2 when God tells Abraham to take "thine *only* son" and offer him as a sacrifice. This word points to Isaac being *one* in an absolute indivisible sense. If the text in Deuteronomy 6:4 had used the word yachid for God, we would have to admit that Judaism, Islam, and even the Jehovah's Witnesses are right and that God is an indivisible unity. We would have to acknowledge that the view that God is a tri-unity and that the Messiah is a divine person is impossible. But it does not. It uses the word echad which opens the possibility that God is a plural unity. It does not prove He is, but the important point here is that it does not prove that He is not.

A fascinating (though somewhat difficult) book on this subject is *The Great Mystery* by Hirsch Prinz. Written in the 19th century, this book quotes extensively from Jewish writings to show that Jewish scholars have long wrestled with the problem of the unity of God as revealed in the Hebrew Bible. He quotes some astonishing writings which point to a view within Judaism of God as a plural unity. He refers to the *memra* (which means *word* in Aramaic) through whom the world was made, also known as "The Middle Pillar" and the Angel of the Covenant (also known as "Metatron" who reveals God to mankind). He writes of a commentary on the Shema (Deuteronomy 6:4) concerning the threefold mention of God's name.[6] I present these quotes, not as an endorsement of everything said but to show the struggle the rabbis have experienced:

> Thus my teacher, Rabbi Simeon ben Jochai, instructed me (Sohar, vol. 3, p. 26) that these three steps in God are three Spirits, each existing of itself, yet united into One. His words are these: "Thus are the three Spirits united in one. The Spirit which is downwards (that is, counting *three*) who is called the Holy Spirit; the Spirit which is the middle pillar, who is called the Spirit of Wisdom and of Understanding, also called the Spirit below. The upper Spirit is hidden in secret; in Him are existing all the holy Spirits (the Holy Spirit and the middle pillar) and all that is light (lit. all faces giving light).[7]

He goes on to show how the ancient paraphrase of the Bible by Jonathan ben Uzziel teaches that it was through the Word (or memra) who is uncreated and self-existing that God created all things:

> That this Word is the essential and uncreated Word, one of the (the Three Heads) which are One, is evident from His being the Creator of man, as the Jerusalem Paraphrase of Jonathan ben Uzziel (Genesis 1:27) faithfully teaches me, saying:

> "And the Word of Jevovah created man in His likeness, in the likeness of Jehovah, Jehovah created, male and female created He them."[8]

He gives a number of references from rabbinic writings to the Divine nature of the Angel of the Covenant or the Angel of God who appeared to the Patriarchs and led the Israelites out of Egypt and through the wilderness. Commenting on Genesis 31:11 ("And the angel of God spake unto me in a dream"), he quotes Rabbi Moses ben Nachman who says:

> According to the truth this Angel, promised here, the Angel, the Redeemer, in whom is the great name; for in the Lord Jehovah is everlasting strength, the Rock of Ages. He is the same, who has said; "I am the God of Beth-el" (Genesis 31:13). The Scriptures have called Him Malach Angel (Ambassador), because through this designation of an Ambassador, we learn that the world is governed through Him.[9]

He quotes extensively from a commentary by Rabbi Bechai on Exodus 23:21 about the Angel of the Lord mentioned above:

> This Angel is not one of those (created) intelligences which can sin . . . this Angel is one of the Inherent Ones. . . . "For He will not pardon your transgressions." Because He belongs to the class of Beings which cannot sin; yea He is Metatron,

the Prince of His (God's) countenance and therefore it is said: "to keep thee in the way."[10]

He goes on to say that this Angel is the one by whom God is made known in the world, who must be obeyed as God must be obeyed and whose power to forgive (or not forgive) sins is not delivered to any of the created intelligences.[11] So if He is uncreated, who is He? This commentary clearly distinguishes between created angels who do have the power to sin and this Angel who is apparently different in nature from any created being.

Developing this theme, he goes on to show how the memra (Word) is not only described as the Angel of God, but also as "Metatron" in rabbinic writings. Concerning this mysterious figure, he quotes Rabbi Simeon ben Yochai in Zohar volume 3 page 227, Amsterdam edition:

> The Middle Pillar (in the Godhead) is the Metatron, who has accomplished peace above, according to the glorious state there.[12]

Rabbi Bechai (Zohar page 114 column 1 Amsterdam edition) says of Metatron:

> God said to Moses, Come up unto the Lord; this is Metatron. He is called by this name Metatron, because in this name are implied two significations, which indicate His character. He is Lord and Messenger. There is also a third idea implied in the name Metatron: it signifies a keeper; for in the Chaldee language, a keeper (or watchman) is called "Matherath"; and because He is the keeper (preserver) of the world, He is called (Psalm 121:4) "The keeper of Israel." From the signification of His name, we learn that He is the Lord over all which is below; because all the hosts of heaven, and all things upon earth, are put under His power and might.[13]

Commenting on Psalm 2, "Thou art my Son; this day have I begotten thee," he quotes "Tikunei Ha Zohar":

> There is a perfect man, who is an Angel. This Angel is Metatron, the keeper of Israel; He is a man in the image of the Holy One, blessed be He, who is an Emanation from Him (God); yea, He, (the Metatron) is Jehovah [Adonai]; of Him [it] cannot be said, He is created, formed or made; but He is the Emanation from God.[14]

A man who is an Angel and who is Adonai, the Lord? If Rabbis can reach this conclusion about the mysterious being we are looking at who appears all over the Hebrew Bible, why should it be considered so impossible that the final revelation of this one should come in Him being born in human form and dwelling amongst us? Is the memra (Word) whom the Rabbis speak of as being active in creation the same one as the *logos* (Word) revealed in John chapter 1—the Word who was made flesh, the one through whom the worlds were made appearing in human form? And since John was a Jewish disciple of Jesus, not a Greek philosopher, is it not much more likely he was thinking of the Rabbinic concept of the memra as he wrote his Gospel, rather than the Greek philosopher Plato's concept of the Logos as is often taught in Christian theological colleges?

Concerning the word memra, this is the phrase used in Jewish writings to speak of how God contracted Himself into a form, able to create the heavens and the earth and also to appear in a form recognizable to humans. When we look at the creation account, we find that God created by speaking the word: "And God said, Let there be light: and there was light." Right through Genesis 1, we have the phrase, "va yomer Elohim"—"And God said." Why does the Bible use this phrase "and God said" when He created the universe? The implication is that there is a creative force to His words which brought the creation into being. God spoke, and it was so. Once the word is uttered, it became whatever God has spoken into being (light, earth, seas, sea creatures, land creatures, birds, human beings). This caused

Jewish thinkers to come up with an explanation as to how God, who is conceived to be "untouchable" and outside of time and space, could create a physical universe. The answer was to provide some kind of link between the invisible God and His creation, which the rabbis called the word or memra from the root of the Hebrew word *imra*—He spoke. In Genesis 1, God spoke the word and the material world came into existence.

We find this memra concept hundreds of times in the Aramaic Targums, the translations and paraphrases of the Hebrew Scriptures that were read in the synagogues before, during, and after the time of Jesus. The Targum for Genesis 1:27, "God created man," reads, "The Word [memra] of the Lord created man." Genesis 3:8 reads, "And they heard the voice of the LORD God walking in the garden;" in the Targum, it reads, "And they heard the sound of the Word [memra] of the Lord God walking in the midst of the garden." Exodus 20:1 (the giving of the Ten Commandments) reads, "And God spake all these words;" in the Targum, it reads, "And the Word [memra] of the Lord spoke all these words." In the Targum of Deuteronomy 4:7, we read, "The Word [memra] of the Lord sits upon his throne high and lifted up and hears our prayer whenever we pray before him and make our petitions." In the Targum, Isaiah 45:17 reads, "Israel will be saved by the Word [memra] of the Lord."

Surely this was the One whom John was thinking of when he opened his Gospel with these words:

> In the beginning was the Word, and the Word was with God, and the Word was God. The same was in the beginning with God. All things were made by him; and without him was not any thing made that was made. In him was life; and the life was the light of men. And the light shineth in darkness; and the darkness comprehended it not. . . . And the Word was made flesh, and dwelt among us, (and we beheld his glory, the glory as of the only begotten of the Father,) full of grace and truth. (John 1:1-5, 14)

CHAPTER 6

CAN WE BELIEVE IN THE VIRGIN BIRTH?

———◆———

In the last chapter, I mentioned Rabbi Kaplan's teaching that "the Jewish Messiah is truly human in origin. He is born of ordinary human parents and is of flesh and blood like all mortals." The New Testament is at pains to make clear there was something very unusual about Jesus' birth, that He was not conceived in the normal way to ordinary human parents. This unusual conception is seen as the fulfillment of Isaiah 7:14:

> Therefore the Lord himself shall give you a sign; Behold, a virgin shall conceive, and bear a son, and shall call his name Immanuel.

So was Jesus born to a virgin, and was this prophesied in Isaiah 7:14?

At a public debate on the issue, "Was Jesus the Messiah?,"[1] Rabbi Shmuley Boteach stated from the platform that any Christian claiming that Isaiah 7:14 is a prophecy of the virgin birth of Jesus is being intellectually dishonest. This means that Christians have to reject the New Testament, since Matthew makes this claim, quoting Isaiah 7:14 in connection with the birth of Jesus and stating:

Now all this was done, that it might be fulfilled which was spoken of the Lord by the prophet, saying, Behold, a virgin shall be with child, and shall bring forth a son, and they shall call his name Emmanuel, which being interpreted is, God with us. (Matthew 1:22-23)

Although Jesus was never called Immanuel in His public life, the New Testament teaches that He was literally "God with us" Immanuel, having both a human and a divine nature.

Jesus also said that details of His life and ministry are prophesied in the Scriptures (i.e. the Tenach or Old Testament):

Search the scriptures; for in them ye think ye have eternal life: and they are they which testify of me. (John 5:39)

Either Jesus is right and the Scriptures written centuries before He came do testify of Him, in which case He is the Messiah and should be listened to, *or* He is wrong and the Scriptures say nothing about Him, in which case He is deluded and should be rejected.

So in order to be intellectually honest in the eyes of Rabbi Boteach, Christians have to reject the New Testament and the words of Jesus, in which case they don't have much left to believe in and might as well reject their faith altogether. Why believe in someone who was deluded and had such an inflated idea of his own importance that he thought words written hundreds of years before he came referred to himself? Why pay attention to a book claiming that Jesus fulfilled prophecies if he did not? If I were to say that the writings of Chaucer or Shakespeare contain prophecies about my life, people would rightly consider me to be mad.

Of course, there are Christians who take Rabbi Boteach's view. Liberal Christian scholarship is at the forefront of undermining the Christian cause from within, and Jewish and Muslim opponents of Christianity like to use their arguments to attack the Christian faith. However, Orthodox Jews like Rabbi Boteach should beware of using the arguments of liberal Christian clergy. The same people who undermine Christian belief in the virgin birth, the miracles of Jesus,

His resurrection, and the second coming, also deny that the Torah is the inspired and infallible Word of God. They undermine belief in the Genesis account of creation, the events of the Exodus, and God's ongoing covenant with Israel.

It is beyond the scope of this book to deal with the debate over the liberal or literal interpretation of the Bible, except to say that the view of Scripture to which I hold is that "[a]ll scripture is given by inspiration of God" (2 Timothy 3:16), and I accept the literal interpretation of historical and prophetic events in Scripture.

ISAIAH 7:14—WHAT ARE THE ISSUES?

There are two major objections to the use of this prophecy in relation to Jesus:

- The Hebrew word *almah* should be translated *young woman*, not virgin.

- The passage in context is a short-term prophecy to King Ahaz about his fears of invasion by an alliance of forces led by Rezin, King of Syria and Pekah, King of Israel, not a prophecy of the virgin birth of the Messiah.

ALMAH (HMLU) OR BETHULAH (HLWTB)?

The main argument relating to this passage is that if the text had meant to stress the virginity of the woman involved, the Hebrew word *bethulah* should have been used rather than the word which is used, almah.

1. While bethulah is used many times in the Bible to mean virgin, there are times when its exclusive use as virgin is questionable. In Genesis 24:16, the passage dealing with Abraham's servant going in search of a bride for Isaac, bethulah is used. It is obviously of the highest importance that Isaac's bride (Rebekah) should be a virgin. The text states: "And the damsel [Hebrew "ha na'ar] was very fair to look upon, a virgin [bethulah]; *neither had any man known her*" (emphasis added). If the word bethulah means virgin exclusively,

the phrase "no man had known her" is unnecessary. It is like saying, "The young woman is a virgin. She has never had sex with a man." The Bible is economical with words and does not waste space with unnecessary phrases. The implication of this added phrase is that bethulah on its own is not a strong enough word to mean that this young woman was definitely a virgin. Therefore, her virginity, which is very important to her eligibility to be Isaac's bride, has to be stated explicitly. Interestingly, almah is used of Rebekah later in the text (Genesis 24:43) by which time her virginity has been demonstrated. There is a similar reference in Judges 21:12 in which the phrase "had known no man" is added to the word bethulah.

2. In Joel 1:8, bethulah is used of a woman mourning for "the husband of her youth." Presumably, therefore, she is no longer a virgin.

3. Bethulah is also used of pagan nations known for their immorality—"O virgin [bethulah] daughter of Babylon" (Isaiah 47:1), "virgin, daughter of Zidon" (Isaiah 23:12), and "O virgin, the daughter of Egypt" (Jeremiah 46:11). In the context, all these nations are facing judgment from God because of their impurity.

I have no doubt that if Isaiah had used bethulah in Isaiah 7:14, Rabbi Boteach would be quoting these Scriptures to demonstrate that the prophet should have used almah if he meant to stress the virginity of the young woman!

The word almah is used seven times in the Bible. Not once does it describe a married woman. In five cases, there is no question about the virginity of the woman involved:

1. Genesis 24:43: Rebekah is clearly an unmarried virgin in this text.

2. Exodus 2:8: So is Miriam in this one.

3. Psalm 68:25: Describing a procession of maidens (unmarried women) playing tambourines in worship of God in the procession

to the Temple. To participate in worship acceptable to God, as described in this Psalm, the maidens (*almoth*—plural of *almah*) would have to be virgins.

4. It is used in Song of Songs 1:3 in contrast to the wives and concubines of Solomon, who would obviously not be virgins.

5. Also in Song of Songs 6:8 in the same way.

A sixth case, which Rabbi Boteach used in the debate about Jesus, is Proverbs 30:18-19:

> There be three things which are too wonderful for me, yea, four which I know not: the way of an eagle in the air; the way of a serpent upon a rock; the way of a ship in the midst of the sea; and the way of a man with a maid [almah].

This verse is followed by verse 20 which says:

> Such is the way of an adulterous woman; she eateth, and wipeth her mouth, and saith, I have done no wickedness.

Rabbi Boteach claimed that verse 20 continues the thought of the previous verse, and therefore the almah referred to is "an adulterous woman" and not a virgin. However, the word used for *wonderful* in verse 18 (*niflu*) implies something positive to follow, not something negative. The structure of Proverbs is one of short sayings, which often contrast with each other rather than follow on from each other. In this case, the adulteress of verse 20 is in contrast to the almah of verse 19.

Now we come to the verse in question, Isaiah 7:14. The root of the word almah implies a sexually mature woman of marriageable age, but who is not yet married. Ancient Jewish culture expected an unmarried woman to be a virgin, as in fact did our own culture until relatively recently. The German word for virgin is *Jungfrau* which literally means *young woman*. In Bible times, a betrothed woman found not to be a virgin was to be put to death according to Deuteronomy 22:13-21.

The Septuagint (Greek translation of the Hebrew Scriptures by Jewish scholars) uses the Greek word *parthenos* to translate almah in Isaiah 7:14. The Septuagint translation was made in about 200 BC by Jewish scholars who obviously had no idea about the Christian claim of the virgin birth of Jesus and who were much closer to the original text in time than we are today. Parthenos only means virgin in Greek, showing that the pre-Christian understanding of Jewish scholars was that this verse refers to a virgin being with child.

In the text, the almah being "with child" would seem to deny her virginity. However, this condition is said to be a sign (*oth*) or miracle given by God. There is nothing miraculous about a young woman being with child in the normal way that would constitute a sign. Moreover, if this was a young unmarried woman being with child by the natural means, this would involve fornication. It is unthinkable that God could give a sign involving sexual immorality. Therefore, there are good grounds for Christians to claim that the word almah is used in this verse to stress the virginity of the person involved, without being intellectually dishonest, as Rabbi Boteach claims.

THE PROPHECY IN CONTEXT—THREE POSSIBLE INTERPRETATIONS

1. It is a short term prophecy to King Ahaz about the threat to his kingdom.

2. It is this, but also a long-term prophecy about the Messiah (i.e. the prophecy has two applications).

3. There are two prophecies, one to King Ahaz about the threat to his kingdom and one to the whole house of David about the birth of the Messiah.

The first option is the one favored by Rabbi Boteach and is used to rule out any further application to the Messiah. The second is the one used by many Christians and implies that Isaiah 7:14 is both a prophecy to King Ahaz and a prophecy of the Messiah. The third is the one we shall look at in this chapter.

BACKGROUND TO THE PASSAGE

To understand this verse, there are two important verses we must look at first.

[A]nd I will put enmity between thee and the woman, and between thy seed and her seed; it shall bruise thy head, and thou shalt bruise his heel. (Genesis 3:15)

According to the earliest Messianic prophecy in the Bible, the "seed" of "the woman" will "bruise" the head of the serpent (i.e., Satan). A crushing blow to the head is fatal, but a blow to the heel is painful, yet not fatal. In other words, a fatal blow will be delivered to Satan, while the one who delivers the blow will suffer in the process, but not fatally. This means that one born of "the woman" is going to bring deliverance to humanity from the power of evil. "The woman" here is a particular woman who will bring forth a particular child. There is even in this prophecy a hint of something supernatural about this birth, since the "seed" (sperm) is provided by the man in sexual reproduction, whereas here the emphasis is on the "seed" of the woman.

From this point on, there are many references to the "seed" in the Bible. God says to Abraham, "In your seed shall all the nations of the earth be blessed" (Genesis 22:18). The promised seed is the Messiah who is to bring blessing to all peoples of the world. His line is traced in the genealogies of the Bible from Adam and Eve through Seth, Noah, Shem, Abraham, Isaac, Jacob, Judah, Jesse, and David (to name some of the most important figures).

Satan hates this "seed" because he knows that Messiah's coming will deal his kingdom a mortal blow. Logically, he will also be hostile to the line of descent and to the individual woman who will bring Him forth. Therefore, he will do everything in his power to prevent this from happening *by trying to eliminate the Messianic line.*

The second verse we must look at is the prophecy to King David through the prophet Nathan:

> And it shall come to pass, when thy days be expired that thou must go to be with thy fathers, that I will raise up thy *seed* after thee, which shall be of thy sons; and I will establish his kingdom. He shall build me an house, and I will stablish his throne for ever. I will be his father, and he shall be my son: and I will not take my mercy away from him, as I took it from him that was before thee: but I will settle him in mine house and in my kingdom for ever: and his throne shall be established for evermore. (1 Chronicles 17:11-14; emphasis added)

On one level, this prophecy speaks of the line of kings that would follow David, but that cannot be the complete fulfillment of the text. It points also to the "seed," the descendant of King David who would be the Messiah.

David's son, King Solomon, ruled for forty years, then died after turning away from the Lord and worshipping foreign gods under the influence of his many wives (1 Kings 11). As a result, the kingdom was divided into the ten tribes under King Jeroboam in the northern kingdom of Israel and the two tribes under Solomon's son, King Rehoboam in the southern kingdom of Judah (1 Kings 12). The northern kingdom of Israel was always out of God's will as Jeroboam ignored the laws of the Torah by setting up calves for worship and making priests of every class of person and having feast days which did not conform to the laws laid down in the Torah (1 Kings 12:26-33).

The southern kingdom of Judah had good and bad kings, but even the bad kings were legitimate rulers according to the promise given to David. There was always the possibility that they could turn back to God under the influence of the prophets and offer the legitimate worship in the Temple through the proper sacrifices and feast days administered by the Levitical priests.

By the time we reach the prophecy of Isaiah 7:14, about 250 years have passed since the division of the united kingdom of David and Solomon into the northern kingdom of Israel (also known as Ephraim) and the southern kingdom of Judah. About twenty years later, the northern kingdom of Israel was to be invaded and carried off into captivity by the Assyrians. For information about the events surrounding the kings mentioned in Isaiah 7, we have to look at 2 Kings 16-17 and 2 Chronicles 28.

Ahaz, the king to whom Isaiah gave the prophecy we are looking at, was one of Judah's worst kings. He turned away from the Lord, worshipped the Baals, the Canaanite gods, and even sacrificed his children to pagan gods in the valley of Hinnom. Because of his wickedness, he was out of God's favor and trouble was coming upon the land in accordance with the general warning given in the Torah to the people of Israel not to worship other gods (Leviticus 26, Deuteronomy 28).

At the beginning of his reign, he suffered defeat at an alliance of Rezin, king of Syria and Pekah, king of Israel, involving loss of territory and life. He was now facing the threat of invasion and a siege of Jerusalem by these two kings who were plotting to depose him. (Isaiah 7:6).

The reason Rezin and Pekah wanted to get rid of Ahaz was that he had made an alliance with Assyria, the rising power to the north of Syria, which was itself threatening to invade Syria and Israel. They wanted Ahaz to join their alliance against Assyria; but he would not, so they planned to put their own puppet king on the throne of Judah, the son of Tabel, who would join with them in their pact against Assyria.

The first part of Isaiah's prophecy (7:3-9) is a message about this situation. Significantly, Isaiah meets Ahaz "at the end of the aqueduct." Why is this detail added? Because it shows that Ahaz was afraid of a coming invasion and siege and so was checking out his water supply (the most vital ingredient in surviving a siege). Isaiah gives him a message that should actually be very encouraging to him. He tells him this attempt to depose him and set up a puppet king by Rezin and Pekah is going to fail.

This plot will not succeed, because if it did, the line of David would cease and, therefore, the promise to David would be null and void. Even more important it would cut off the Messianic line. The historical books of the Bible show that God took pains to preserve the line of David despite their continual failings. Concerning a later king, Jehoram who "did evil in the sight of the LORD" we read:

> Howbeit the LORD would not destroy the house of David, because of the covenant that he had made with David, and as he promised to give a light to him and to his sons for ever. (2 Chronicles 21:7)

Despite the fact that Isaiah's message to Ahaz should be an encouragement to him, God knows that he is a man full of unbelief and is trusting in his own plans to get himself out of the hole he was in. So the last part of Isaiah 7:9 has a personal message to Ahaz. "If you will not believe, surely you will not be established." If he were to turn to God in faith he would find security, but not if he continues in unbelief.

Ahaz had his own reasons for not wanting to hear what Isaiah was saying. He was secretly making a pact with the king of Assyria to defend him against Rezin and Pekah. This was like using the Devil to fight against the demons because Assyria was going to turn out to be a much more ferocious and deadly foe of the kingdom of Judah than Syria and Israel ever were. What Ahaz should have done is trust in God, as his own son Hezekiah was to do when faced with a similar threat to his kingdom (Isaiah 36-37).

God then offers to give Ahaz a sign to confirm the message that Isaiah is giving him. A sign (Hebrew word "oth") would show there is a supernatural God in control of events who is infinitely more powerful than puny men, no matter how powerful they seem to be. At this point Ahaz puts on an act of being pious. He is being confronted by the living God, but he does not want to face God. That would disturb his plans. So he gets religious and says, "I will not ask, neither will I tempt the LORD" (Isaiah 7:12).

His refusal of the sign offered in verse 11 is a reference to Deuteronomy 6:16, "Ye shall not tempt [or put to the test] the LORD your God." However, as often happens when unbelievers quote Scripture to justify themselves, this is a misquote. God does not want us to look for a sign or demand a sign, but if He is offering a sign, we are to take it.

Up until this point, the prophecy has been entirely directed to Ahaz and his immediate situation. In the Hebrew, it is clear there is a change in verse 13, which is not clear in our translations, apart from the *King James Version*. From verse 4-11, the word for *you* has been in the singular. In other words, God has been talking to one man, Ahaz. He has not been listening though. His failure to listen to God is not just his problem. It is the problem of most of the kings of the house of David.

From verse 13-14 the prophecy is addressed to "you" in the plural. Now God is talking to the whole house of David, and telling them that He is pretty fed up with them! Whether they want it or not, He is going to give them a sign which will give the deeper reason as to why, despite their obvious failures, He is going to preserve them until the appointed time. The sign is the key verse:

> Behold a virgin shall conceive, and bear a son, and shall call His name Immanuel. (Isaiah 7:14)

Because of the Messianic prophecy of the seed of the woman (Genesis 3:15) and the promise to David that he would have a descendant who would have an eternal throne, God is going to preserve the line of David and keep Ahaz on the throne. Even though he is a wicked king, he is in the line of succession, unlike the son of Tabel. There is a possibility that even if he does not repent, his son who comes after him may repent and follow the Lord (as Hezekiah in fact did).

There is a further important reason why God had to preserve the kingdom under Ahaz in order for the Messiah to come forth. When the Assyrians eventually overran the northern kingdom of Israel (2 Kings 17) they took the people into captivity, where they intermarried and lost their identity as Jews, never again to return to the land of Israel (although there were members of all the tribes of Israel living in Judah who survived this deportation. See 2 Chronicles 11:13-17, 15:9). By the way, they did not migrate northwards to become British, as the strange belief of British Israelism teaches!

If the southern kingdom of Judah had been taken into captivity by the Assyrians, the Jewish people would have disappeared and the promise of the Messiah would have never come to pass. So God rescued Judah from the invading Assyrians (2 Kings 18-19). On one level this was because of the ministry of Isaiah the prophet and the response to Isaiah's teaching by Ahaz's successor, King Hezekiah. On a deeper level it was in order to preserve the Jewish people in the Promised Land until the coming of the Messiah.

In Isaiah 8, we read a prophecy of the coming Assyrian invasion and the word of the Lord that it will fail to overrun Judah. The reason is given in Isaiah 8:10, "it shall not stand: for God is with us." This verse can be understood on two levels. On the first level, God is with Judah through the covenant made with Abraham and with David, so He will defend His people. But the verse could also be translated "It will fail because of Immanuel." This points to the second level at which this verse can be understood. The Assyrian invasion will come to nothing because God will preserve the Jewish people for the coming of Immanuel, the one to be born to "the woman" by virgin birth several centuries later.

When eventually the southern kingdom of Judah was invaded and deported some 150 years later, the Assyrian Empire had been overthrown by the Babylonian Empire. The Babylonians had a different policy towards conquered people and kept them separate, without intermarriage, thus preserving the identity of the Jewish people. The Babylonian Empire was then overthrown by the Medes and the Persians (Daniel 5). They had a different policy again, which meant that the Persian King Cyrus made an edict for the exiled peoples to return and resettle their lands (Ezra 1:1-4). Therefore, the Jewish people were able to return to Israel and rebuild Jerusalem and the Temple, thus preserving the line of David and living in the Promised Land until the coming of the Messiah. One of the leaders of the returning people was Zerubbabel, a descendant of Jeconiah, the last of the kings of Judah in the line of David. His name is recorded in the genealogy of Jesus in chapter one of Matthew.

In this light, the Immanuel prophecy of Isaiah 7:14 had a definite relevance to King Ahaz and the whole of the line of kings in succession to David. It was that God would preserve them despite their failure to keep His ways until His appointed time, in order to bring forth the Messiah who would be the "seed of the woman" born in a supernatural way by virgin birth.

Following the virgin birth prophecy, God goes back to speaking directly to Ahaz and from verse 15 onwards the word *you* goes back to the singular. A prophecy concerning the future conception and birth of the Messiah about 700 years later was interesting but not much use to Ahaz in his immediate predicament. Isaiah now tells him that both the kings threatening him (Rezin and Pekah) will be removed from power themselves "before the child shall know to refuse the evil and choose the good" (i.e. reach the age of maturity when he can make independent moral judgments).

The question now has to be asked, "Which child is this prophecy referring to?" Because the Hebrew is "*the* child" not "*a* child," it must be referring back to a child who is either already mentioned in the text or one who is already known to the hearers of the prophecy. In Isaiah 7, there are two references to boys: Immanuel in verse 14, and Shear-jashub, Isaiah's son in verse 3. Which one is referred to here?

The most common interpretation is that it refers to Immanuel. In other words, there was a boy called Immanuel who was to be born about this time. Before he was old enough to know good from evil, the two kings Ahaz was afraid of would no longer be a threat to him. Christian commentators who say that the prophecy has two applications, one to Ahaz and one to the birth of Jesus, interpret it this way saying it applies both to this boy called Immanuel and to the birth of Jesus.

However, there are difficulties with this. For one thing if we take the dates given in 2 Kings 16-17, King Pekah of Israel was assassinated three years after Ahaz came to the throne. This means that the prophecy of Isaiah 7 must have been given to Ahaz at the beginning of his reign and the outcome of the prophecy would take place in a short time, much less time than was needed for a child to be born and reach the age of maturity.

A better interpretation is given by Arnold Fruchtenbaum in which he says that the boy referred to in Isaiah 7:16 is not Immanuel, but Shear-Jashub, Isaiah's young son, who was standing there before Ahaz at the time the prophecy was given.[2] This explains why Isaiah was told by the Lord to take his son with him, even though that might be a dangerous thing to do. Isaiah's son's name is also relevant to the whole issue of this prophecy. It means "a remnant shall return" pointing to the coming deportation of Judah to Babylon and the remnant who would return from this captivity to continue the line of David living in the Promised Land until the coming of the Messiah.

Later in Ahaz's reign the threat to his kingdom from Israel and Syria receded. Pekah, king of Israel, was assassinated by Hoshea in the third year of Ahaz's reign (2 Kings 15:30). Five years after the death of Ahaz, in the ninth year of Hoshea, King of Israel, the Assyrians invaded Syria and the northern kingdom of Israel, taking its people into captivity (2 Kings 17). God supernaturally prevented them from taking Judah into captivity as well, in response to Isaiah's ministry and in order to fulfill His prophetic word concerning the coming Messiah (2 Kings 18-19).

So there are two prophecies. There is a short-term prophecy concerning events which were soon to be fulfilled given to King Ahaz. There is a long-term prophecy concerning the miraculous conception and birth of the son who would be Immanuel, God with us, to be fulfilled in Yeshua, Jesus the Messiah, given to the whole House of David.

CONCLUSION

As a result of all this, the Messianic line was preserved and the Jewish people continued in the land of Israel until the time of the fulfillment of the Immanuel prophecy in the birth of the Messiah Jesus. Forty years after His crucifixion, the Romans destroyed Jerusalem and the Temple, dispersed the Jewish people and caused the genealogical records in the Temple to be destroyed. Therefore, Messiah had to come before this event in order to show His descent from David. The prophecy of Daniel 9:26 indicates that Messiah would come and be "cut off" before the destruction of the Second Temple, giving another pointer to His identity since, according to this prophecy, the Messiah had to come before 70 AD when the Temple was destroyed.

Concerning the prophecy itself it refers to a future conception and birth of a son. This is to be a sign, a miraculous event, something involving divine intervention. The son is to be born to a woman of marriageable age, but she herself could not be married because she had to be a virgin. As I have already said, for God to give a sign of a birth conceived by an act of fornication would be unthinkable.

The woman herself is referred to as "*the* woman/virgin" not "*a* woman." Commenting on this, Arnold Fruchtenbaum writes:

> According to the rules of Hebrew grammar, when finding the use of a definite article (*the*), the reader should look back for a reference in the immediate previous context. Having followed the passage from chapter 7:1, there has been no mention of any woman. Having failed with the immediate context, the second rule is the "principle of previous reference," something which has been dealt with much earlier and is common knowledge among the people. Where in Jewish Scripture is there any concept of "the virgin giving birth to a son"? The only possible reference is to Genesis 3:15 (the "seed of the woman" prophecy referred to above). Contrary to the biblical norm, the Messiah would be reckoned after the Seed of the Woman. Why? Because He would have no human father; His would be a virgin conception and birth.[3]

The only possible way this prophecy could be fulfilled is the event described in the Gospels, the virgin birth of the Messiah. The angel Gabriel arrives to speak to "a virgin espoused to a man whose name was Joseph, of the house of David" (Luke 1:27). Mary (Miriam) is "highly favoured . . . among women" because she is "the woman" of Genesis 3:15. She has to be unmarried and therefore a virgin. She also has to be betrothed to be married because if she were to come out of this experience as an unmarried mother, her position in society and the position of her son would be very difficult indeed.

It is vital that her intended husband does not reject her when he discovers that she is pregnant. So the angel also speaks to Joseph to ensure that he goes ahead with the marriage despite Mary's condition

(Matthew 1:20-25). In order to explain this to Joseph, he is made aware of the prophecy of Isaiah 7:14 concerning the virgin birth. Mary is treated with great honor in the New Testament (although never worshipped or elevated to be "Queen of Heaven"*), but Joseph, too, acts with great faith and integrity, playing a vital role in bringing the Messiah into the world.

Both Joseph and Mary are of the line of David, with Joseph's genealogy given in Matthew 1 through the royal line of the kings, and Mary's genealogy given in Luke 3 through a different son of David, Nathan. Although the text of Luke 3 speaks of "Joseph the son of Heli," this lines up with the convention of not putting the female name, and this genealogy is really Mary's. The Talmud actually refers to Miriam (Mary) *bat* (daughter of) Heli.[4]

Having established the connection to the line of David (Luke 1:27), the angel Gabriel says to Mary:

> And, behold, thou shalt conceive in thy womb, and bring forth a son, and shalt call his name JESUS. He shall be great, and shall be called the Son of the Highest: and the Lord God shall give unto him the throne of his father David: and he shall reign over the house of Jacob for ever; and of his kingdom there shall be no end. (Luke 1:31-33)

It can be no accident that the three eternal things promised to David of his "seed" in 1 Chronicles 17:11-14—an eternal *throne*, an eternal *house* and an eternal *kingdom*—are prophesied here of the "seed" of Mary who was to be conceived supernaturally by the Holy Spirit:

> The Holy Ghost shall come upon thee, and the power of the Highest shall overshadow thee: therefore also that holy

---

*Read Roger Oakland's book *Queen of All* to gain an understanding of this title that has been wrongly given to Mary.

thing which shall be born of thee shall be called the Son of God. (Luke 1:35)

It is nothing for God to overrule the laws of nature in order to bring His purposes to fulfillment:

For with God nothing shall be impossible. (Luke 1:37)

This passage gives the key to a problem which is as yet unresolved by this investigation of the virgin birth prophecy. From a human point of view without reference to any fulfillment in Jesus, the promise given to David in 1 Chronicles 17 was a false prophecy. There is no king of the line of David alive on Earth today and has not been for over 2500 years. Jeconiah was the last descendant of David to sit on Judah's throne. According to the prophecy of Jeremiah 22:30 after Jeconiah there would be no king descended from David again (the actual last king before the Babylonian captivity, Zedekiah, was Jeconiah's uncle not his son).

Moreover, if the prophecy of 1 Chronicles 17 is just about the human descendants of David, it is impossible to fulfill. It speaks of an eternal house, throne, and kingdom which the prophesied descendant of David will inherit. But no mere man can have these things *eternally*. The only way that could happen is if the one it speaks of is Himself an eternal person, i.e. Immanuel—God with us.

The relevance of all this to Isaiah 7 is crucial. God's covenant with David concerning his descendants is to go beyond the line of kings, which would follow him and to reach its fulfillment in the supernatural birth of the Messiah. The Messiah is to do mortal damage to Satan's kingdom; therefore Satan will do all that he can to prevent the fulfillment of this prophecy. Because God is greater than Satan, He will ensure that His purposes are fulfilled, preserving the line of David in some identifiable form until Messiah comes and keeping the Jewish people in the land of Israel until this time.

The Holy Spirit would overshadow a virgin betrothed to be married who would give birth to a son who would be more than just a man. He would be Immanuel, God with us. God would enter human existence in the person of Yeshua, Jesus the Messiah. In this way, He would be both Son of Man and Son of God, without sin and, therefore, able to be the perfect sacrifice required to redeem lost humanity.

The New Testament shows how Messiah was born in this supernatural way in order to redeem us from our sins. It is nothing for God to overrule the laws of nature, which He Himself has set up, and bring forth a son without a human father. This was God's way of coming into the world, to take on human form. He continues to be with us as the mediator who brings us into a relationship with God.

He is able right now to give us peace and security, even if we face enemies coming against us as King Ahaz did. Ahaz was not established on David's throne, nor in the kingdom of God, because he lacked faith in the promises of God. But we can have absolute faith in the promises of God revealed in Messiah Jesus. All of this and much more is fulfilled in Messiah Jesus who has come once in fulfillment of prophecy and is coming again to complete the Messianic program and rule on David's throne.

To believe in Him, you do not have to be intellectually dishonest, but you do have to have the courage to go against the flow and to stand firm in the face of adversity, unlike King Ahaz, but like his son King Hezekiah, who believed and was established both on David's throne and in the kingdom of God.

CHAPTER 7

THE SUFFERING SERVANT

———◆———

WHO IS THIS PROPHET TALKING ABOUT?

The other big issue coming out of Isaiah's prophecy centers on this passage in Isaiah:

Behold, my servant shall deal prudently, he shall be exalted and extolled, and be very high. As many were astonied [astonished] at thee; his visage was so marred more than any man, and his form more than the sons of men: So shall he sprinkle many nations; the kings shall shut their mouths at him: for that which had not been told them shall they see; and that which they had not heard shall they consider.

Who hath believed our report? and to whom is the arm of the LORD revealed? For he shall grow up before him as a tender plant, and as a root out of a dry ground: he hath no form nor comeliness; and when we shall see him, there is no beauty that we should desire him. He is despised and rejected of men; a man of sorrows, and acquainted with grief: and we hid as it were our faces from him; he was despised, and we esteemed him not.

Surely he hath borne our griefs, and carried our sorrows: yet we did esteem him stricken, smitten of God, and afflicted. But he was wounded for our transgressions, he was bruised for our iniquities: the chastisement of our peace was upon him; and with his stripes we are healed. All we like sheep have gone astray; we have turned every one to his own way; and the LORD hath laid on him the iniquity of us all.

He was oppressed, and he was afflicted, yet he opened not his mouth: he is brought as a lamb to the slaughter, and as a sheep before her shearers is dumb, so he openeth not his mouth. He was taken from prison and from judgment: and who shall declare his generation? for he was cut off out of the land of the living: for the transgression of my people was he stricken.

And he made his grave with the wicked, and with the rich in his death; because he had done no violence, neither was any deceit in his mouth. Yet it pleased the LORD to bruise him; he hath put him to grief: when thou shalt make his soul an offering for sin, he shall see his seed, he shall prolong his days, and the pleasure of the LORD shall prosper in his hand. He shall see of the travail of his soul, and shall be satisfied: by his knowledge shall my righteous servant justify many; for he shall bear their iniquities.

Therefore will I divide him a portion with the great, and he shall divide the spoil with the strong; because he hath poured out his soul unto death: and he was numbered with the transgressors; and he bare the sin of many, and made intercession for the transgressors. (Isaiah 52:13-53:12)

Who is the prophet talking about?

- Himself?
- Someone else?
- Israel?
- The Messiah?

WHAT IF ISAIAH 53 IS ABOUT ISRAEL?

According to Rashi, a French rabbinical scholar who lived from 1040 to 1105 and wrote a very influential commentary on the Bible and on the Talmud, the answer is clear. The prophet is talking about Israel suffering for the Gentiles. Today, the almost universal view taken by Rabbis is that this is the Jewish interpretation of Isaiah 53.

However, according to Arnold Fruchtenbaum:

> Every rabbi prior to Rashi, without exception, viewed this passage as describing Messiah. When Rashi first proposed that this passage spoke of the nation of Israel, he sparked a fierce debate with his contemporaries. The most famous of these was Rambam, better known as Maimonides. Rambam stated very clearly that Rashi is completely wrong and going against the traditional Jewish viewpoint.[1]

The Targum is an ancient paraphrase of the Bible by Jonathan ben Uzziel from the first century. His Targums were often quoted by early Rabbis, and he was considered an authority on the Jewish view of the Bible. His Targum of Isaiah 52:13 clearly connects this passage to the Messiah, saying, "Behold my servant Messiah will prosper."[2]

A prayer written by Rabbi Eliezer Kalir for the afternoon service of Yom Kippur (Day of Atonement) in around the 7th century reads:

> Messiah our righteousness is departed from us; horror hath seized us, and we have none to justify us. He hath borne the yoke of our iniquities, and our transgression and is wounded because of our transgression. He bears our sin upon his shoulder, that He may find pardon for our iniquities. We shall be healed by his wound at the time the Eternal will create Him (the Messiah) as a new creature. O bring Him up from the circle of the earth. Raise Him up from Seir, to assemble us the second time on Mount Lebanon, by the hand of Yinnon.[3]

This prayer quotes from Isaiah 53 and connects this passage to Messiah who "bears our sin" and who has "departed from us," which has become a matter of horror because now "we have none to justify us." Yinnon is a name for Messiah, so the prayer even speaks of Messiah coming a second time to "assemble us."

Rabbi Moshe Cohen Ibn Crispin of Cordova in Spain at about 1350 wrote about Isaiah 53 in a refutation of Rashi's view:

> [I shall be free from] the forced and far-fetched interpretations, of which others have been guilty. . . . This prophecy was delivered by Isaiah at the divine command for the purpose of making known to us something about the nature of the future Messiah, who is to come and deliver Israel.[4]

Rabbi Alshech wrote in about 1550 about Isaiah 53:

> [O]ur Rabbis with one voice accept and affirm the opinion that the prophet is speaking of the King Messiah, and we shall ourselves also adhere to the same view.[5]

Rabbi Eliyahu de Vidas wrote in about 1575 that not only is Isaiah 53 about the Messiah, but those who refuse to believe this must suffer for their sins themselves:

> *But He was wounded for our transgressions, bruised for our iniquities,* the meaning of which is that since the Messiah bears our iniquities which produce the effect of his being bruised, it follows that whoso will not admit that the Messiah thus suffers for our iniquities must endure and suffer for them himself.[6]
> (emphasis in original)

All these Rabbis are saying that Isaiah 53 is about Messiah suffering for sin, *not* about Israel suffering on behalf of the Gentiles.

So is Rashi right when he says Isaiah 53 is a prophecy about Israel suffering for the Gentiles? If so, are those Rabbis who claim this is about the sufferings of the Messiah wrong? If we examine the text, Rashi's interpretation raises some questions because it would mean that:

‖ Isaiah is a Gentile.

Verses 5 and 6 have to mean the following: "He [Israel] was wounded for our transgressions." "All we [Gentiles] like sheep have gone astray . . . and the LORD hath laid on him [Israel] the iniquity of us all." In the passage, the pronouns we, us, and our must refer to Isaiah and the people he identifies with, while the pronouns he, him, his refer to the "servant." In this case, the people with whom Isaiah identifies are Gentiles, and the people identified with the servant are Israel. So was Isaiah 53 written by a Gentile?

‖ Israel bears the sins of the Gentiles in some kind of atoning way.

So what did Isaiah mean in the first chapter of his prophecy when he spoke in the strongest language imaginable about Israel's sins and called his own people to repentance?

> Ah sinful nation, a people laden with iniquity, a seed of evildoers, children that are corrupters: they have forsaken the LORD, they have provoked the Holy One of Israel. (Isaiah 1:4)

How can someone who is sinful bear the sins of others?

In reality, Israel suffers *because of* the sins of the Gentiles not on *behalf of* the Gentiles. Gentiles who reject the true understanding of God and the Messiah have often persecuted the Jewish people. But this does no good to the Gentiles responsible and puts them under God's curse according to Genesis 12:3 "And I will bless them that bless thee, and curse him that curseth thee." There is no way that anti-Semitism brings any good on those responsible, but the servant of Isaiah 53 offers justification and healing even to those responsible for His suffering, provided they turn to Him that He may bear their iniquities (verse 11).

Rashi's interpretation implies that Jewish people are sin bearers for the Gentiles. That lines up in a way with the stereotype which Gentile anti-Semites have put on the Jewish people making them the scapegoats who are responsible for all that is wrong in their own society. Another point on this issue is that Jewish people have never willingly suffered at the hands of Gentiles, whereas the Servant of Isaiah 53 offers Himself of His own will as a sacrifice.

‖ Israel/the Jewish people will cease to live.

The servant of Isaiah 53 is literally put to death. "[H]e was cut off out of the land of the living" (v 8). "[H]e hath poured out his soul unto death" (v 12). Individual Jewish people have been put to death. In the Holocaust, a demon-inspired leader sought to destroy the whole Jewish people. But despite the evil intentions of anti-Semites—*"Am Israel Chai"*—The people of Israel live. This fulfills the prophecy of Jeremiah 31:35-37, which says that as long as the sun, moon, and stars endure, so long will Israel be a nation before the Lord. The servant of Isaiah 53 dies and is resurrected to "see of the travail of his soul." The Jewish people have never ceased to exist and, therefore, do not need to be resurrected as a whole people.

WHAT IF ISAIAH 53 IS ABOUT THE MESSIAH?

So far, we have treated this as a debate within Judaism about different rabbinic interpretations, which may be interesting, but not in itself earth shattering. But if Rashi is wrong and the prophecy is not about Israel suffering for the nations and it is about the Messiah, there remains an interpretation which does raise a very big problem for Judaism.

The prayer of Rabbi Kalir quoted above speaks of Messiah as one who has departed from us and who bears our sins and who will bring us healing. Rabbi Eliyahu de Vidas tells us that whoever does not believe that Messiah suffers for our iniquities, "must endure and suffer for them himself."

If the Messiah has "departed from us" does that mean that He has already appeared? Is there a figure in history who has already borne the sins of others? If we do not believe in Him, do we have to endure and suffer for our sins ourselves?

The New Testament claims that Jesus' sufferings on the Cross are the fulfillment of Isaiah 53. Does this interpretation make sense of the text? We invite you to study this text and look up the references given in the New Testament.

ISAIAH 52:13-15

These verses introduce the Servant who is described in detail in the verses that follow. The servant will be exalted very high. Prior to His exaltation, He was to be humiliated and physically abused to the point where He became almost unrecognizable. As a result, He would "sprinkle many nations" (vs. 15) and kings would be silent before Him.

The crucifixion account is brief and graphic:

> And so Pilate, willing to content the people, released Barabbas unto them, and delivered Jesus, when he had scourged him, to be crucified. And the soldiers led him away into the hall, called Praetorium; and they call together the whole band. And they clothed him with purple, and platted a crown of thorns, and put it about his head, And began to salute him, Hail, King of the Jews! And they smote him on the head with a reed, and did spit upon him, and bowing their knees worshipped him. And when they had mocked him, they took off the purple from him, and put his own clothes on him, and led him out to crucify him. And they compel one Simon a Cyrenian, who passed by, coming out of the country, the father of Alexander and Rufus, to bear his cross. And they bring him unto the place Golgotha, which is, being interpreted, The place of a skull.

And they gave him to drink wine mingled with myrrh: but he received it not. And when they had crucified him, they parted his garments, casting lots upon them, what every man should take. And it was the third hour, and they crucified him. And the superscription of his accusation was written over, THE KING OF THE JEWS. (Mark 15:15-26)

Anyone going through this level of physical abuse and humiliation would become almost unrecognizable as Isaiah prophesied. Yet despite this humiliation, He was to be raised to life again and ascend to the highest place, just as Isaiah said He would be. Peter explains this in his speech on the Day of Pentecost:

Ye men of Israel, hear these words; Jesus of Nazareth, a man approved of God among you by miracles and wonders and signs, which God did by him in the midst of you, as ye yourselves also know: Him, being delivered by the determinate counsel and foreknowledge of God, ye have taken, and by wicked hands have crucified and slain: Whom God hath raised up, having loosed the pains of death: because it was not possible that he should be holden of it. For David speaketh concerning him,

I foresaw the Lord always before my face, for he is on my right hand, that I should not be moved: Therefore did my heart rejoice, and my tongue was glad; moreover also my flesh shall rest in hope: Because thou wilt not leave my soul in hell, neither wilt thou suffer thine Holy One to see corruption. Thou hast made known to me the ways of life; thou shalt make me full of joy with thy countenance. [Psalm 16:8-11]

Men and brethren, let me freely speak unto you of the patriarch David, that he is both dead and buried, and his sepulchre is with us unto this day. Therefore being a prophet, and knowing that God had sworn with an oath to him, that of the fruit of his loins, according to the flesh, he would raise up Christ to sit on his throne; He seeing this before spake of the resurrection of Christ, that his soul was not left in hell, neither his flesh did see corruption. This Jesus hath God raised up, whereof we all are witnesses. Therefore being by the right hand of God exalted, and having received of the Father the promise of the Holy Ghost, he hath shed forth this, which ye now see and hear. For David is not ascended into the heavens: but he saith himself,

The Lord said unto my Lord, Sit thou on my right hand, Until I make thy foes thy footstool. [Psalm 110:1]

Therefore let all the house of Israel know assuredly, that God hath made the same Jesus, whom ye have crucified, both Lord and Christ. (Acts 2:22-36)

Isaiah 52:15 also speaks about the servant "sprinkling" many nations. This is the teaching of the New Testament that the blood of Jesus replaces the blood of the animal sacrifices as the means whereby God can forgive our sins:

But Christ [Messiah] being come an high priest of good things to come, by a greater and more perfect tabernacle, not made with hands, that is to say, not of this building; Neither by the blood of goats and calves, but by his own blood he entered in once into the holy place, having obtained eternal redemption for us. For if the blood of bulls and of goats, and the ashes of an heifer sprinkling the unclean, sanctifieth to the purifying of the flesh: How much more shall the blood of Christ, who through the eternal Spirit offered himself without spot to God, purge your conscience from dead works to serve the living God? And for this cause he is the mediator of the new testament, that by means of death, for the redemption of the transgressions that were under the first testament, they which are called might receive the promise of eternal inheritance. (Hebrews 9:11-15)

This then is the message which we have heard of him, and declare unto you, that God is light, and in him is no darkness at all. If we say that we have fellowship with him, and walk in darkness, we lie, and do not the truth: But if we walk in the light, as he is in the light, we have fellowship one with another, and the blood of Jesus Christ his Son cleanseth us from all sin. (1 John 1:5-7)

ISAIAH 53:1-3

These verses speak of the rejection which would accompany the ministry of this servant. His message would not be believed. His origin and appearance would not meet the expectations of the people, and therefore, they would reject Him. This rejection would cause Him grief.

The New Testament records the rejection of Jesus throughout the time of His public ministry for precisely these reasons. He was rejected by those who thought He was born in Nazareth, not in Bethlehem— the place prophesied for the coming Messiah (Micah 5:1, John 1:46, John 7:40-44, John 9:29, John 12:37-41). He was rejected by His own family and the people with whom He had grown up, who said of Him "Is not this the carpenter's son?" (See Matthew 13:55, Luke 4:16-30). He was rejected by the religious leaders who objected to the miracles He did on the Sabbath (John 9:16), His association with people they considered to be sinners (Matthew 9:11, Luke 15), and above all be- cause of His claim to be equal with God (Matthew 26:65, Mark 2:7, John 8:58, John 10:30). He was even rejected at His hour of need by the disciples who could not stay awake to pray with Him at the time of His arrest (Matthew 26:36-46), and who ran away and left Him, even denying to know Him (Mark 14:27-72). On the cross, He was even rejected by the Father as the sins of the world were placed upon Him. This was why He quoted the words of the Messianic Psalm 22, "My God, my God, why hast thou forsaken me?" (Matthew 27:46).

In all of this, Jesus experienced grief just as Isaiah said the Servant would:

> And he took with him Peter and the two sons of Zebedee, and began to be sorrowful and very heavy. Then saith he unto them, My soul is exceeding sorrowful, even unto death. (Matthew 26:37-38)

ISAIAH 53:4-6

These verses take the sufferings of the Servant further and describe the purpose of His suffering. His death would be misinterpreted by those who said He was stricken by God and afflicted (in other words He was suffering for His own sins). In fact, the whole meaning of His sufferings was to atone for the sins of others. Because He experienced the worst sorrows life can throw at anyone, He can sympathize and carry the griefs of those who are going through suffering now. The Lord has placed on Him the iniquity of us all so that we can be forgiven.

Jesus was accused of blasphemy and treason against Rome and executed as a common criminal. The Roman governor responsible had the mocking sign, "Jesus of Nazareth, King of the Jews" placed above the cross, which ironically contained the truth about who Jesus was. However, his intention was to mock both Jesus and the Jewish people whom he despised. The religious leaders also mocked Him and implied that His execution was His own fault for making false claims to be the Messiah and the King of Israel (Mark 14-15). Even today scoffers say "Jesus suffered for his own sins, not mine."

Yet every person who turns to Jesus in sincerity discovers that He is able to forgive their sins and give them eternal life. The reason for the death of Jesus is made plain in the New Testament:

> For the Son of man is come to seek and to save that which was lost. (Luke 19:10)

> For God so loved the world, that he gave his only begotten Son, that whosoever believeth in him should not perish, but

have everlasting life. For God sent not his Son into the world to condemn the world; but that the world through him might be saved. (John 3:16-17)

Christ [Messiah] also suffered for us, leaving us an example, that ye should follow his steps: who did no sin, neither was guile found in his mouth: who, when he was reviled, reviled not again; when he suffered, he threatened not; but committed himself to him that judgeth righteously: who his own self bare our sins in his own body on the tree, that we, being dead to sins, should live unto righteousness: by whose stripes ye were healed. For ye were as sheep going astray; but are now returned unto the Shepherd and Bishop of your souls. (1 Peter 2:21-25)

ISAIAH 53:7-9

These verses tell us about the sufferings of the Messiah from a human point of view. He would be brought to trial and willingly accept the death sentence handed down to Him, despite its injustice. He would be literally put to death and once again it is stated that His death would be for the sins of "my people." Although He would be expected to be put in a grave with the wicked, there would be some intervention of "the rich" at the point of His death.

Jesus' trials before Caiaphas and Pontius Pilate were both unfair and a denial of both Jewish and Roman law.

Now the chief priests, and elders, and all the council, sought false witness against Jesus, to put him to death; but found none. (Matthew 26:59-60)

Jesus did not try to defend Himself, knowing that it was necessary for Him to go to the cross in order to redeem the world.

And when he was accused of the chief priests and elders, he answered nothing. Then said Pilate unto him, Hearest thou not how many things they witness against thee? And he answered him to never a word; insomuch that the governor marvelled greatly. (Matthew 27:12-14)

The Roman soldiers who had witnessed countless similar executions were in no doubt that Jesus was dead before He was taken down from the cross (John 19:32-35). What happened next is very interesting in the light of Isaiah's prophecy. The usual practice was for crucifixion victims to stay on the cross as a warning to others not to go against the power of the occupying Romans or for their bodies to be taken down and thrown into a common grave in the Valley of Hinnom outside Jerusalem. If either had happened to Jesus, the next event, the resurrection, would have lost its force.

So God caused a rich man, Joseph of Arimathea, to intervene and ask Pontius Pilate for the body of Jesus so he could bury Him in his own tomb (Matthew 27:57-60). Pilate agreed to this, perhaps influenced by his wife's dream not to have anything to do with "that just man" (Matthew 27:19), perhaps because of Roman superstitions about Jesus as a miracle worker (the Roman authorities would have known that Jesus had raised Lazarus from the dead) (John 11:47-48). The body of Jesus was placed in a sealed tomb with a stone rolled across it, so when the resurrection happened it was much easier to verify or discredit the story than it would have been if the body had been thrown into a common grave. It therefore became much more difficult to take seriously the rumors that the disciples had stolen the body (Matthew 28). It would have been relatively easy for the authorities to show this rumor was true and thereby discredit the whole Messianic movement if they could have produced the body of Jesus, thus showing that the disciples were liars. Less than two months later, the disciples were preaching in Jerusalem that Jesus was risen from the dead and facing opposition, imprisonment, and even death for doing so. You don't do that for a story you have made up.

ISAIAH 53:10-12

These verses tell us the purpose of the Servant's death and speak of His resurrection from the dead. He would be satisfied by seeing His "seed" and would bring justification to many by bearing their iniquities. God would highly exalt Him because He was willing to be considered a transgressor and die. He would make intercession for transgressors.

As we have already seen in Chapter 2, the ultimate responsibility for the death of Jesus is with God. Isaiah 53:10 tells us that "it pleased the Lord to bruise him; he hath put him to grief." The New Testament agrees entirely with this and places responsibility for Jesus' death on the sins of the world and the will of God (Acts 4:25-28). His death was to be literal, as Jesus' death was, and yet He would "see his seed . . . and shall be satisfied" (Isaiah 53:10-11). How can this be possible? The only way is because He rises from the dead. Jesus explained this to the disciples and then commissioned them to go into all the world and tell people about Him. In this way, others would come to know Him, and He would be satisfied as He saw that all the pain of the cross was worthwhile because it would bring multitudes of people all over the world into the kingdom of God:

> And he said unto them, These are the words which I spake unto you, while I was yet with you, that all things must be fulfilled, which were written in the law of Moses, and in the prophets, and in the psalms, concerning me.
>
> Then opened he their understanding, that they might understand the scriptures, and said unto them, Thus it is written, and thus it behoved Christ to suffer, and to rise from the dead the third day: and that repentance and remission of sins should be preached in his name among all nations, beginning at Jerusalem. And ye are witnesses of these things. And, behold, I send the promise of my Father upon you: but tarry ye in the city of Jerusalem, until ye be endued with power from on high. (Luke 24:44-49)

The Book of Acts records the spread of the Gospel beginning in Jerusalem and then going out to "Judea and Samaria" and to the ends of the Earth. In this way, multitudes of people would be justified, put right with God:

> [B]ut now in Christ [Messiah] Jesus ye who sometimes were far off are made nigh by the blood of Christ. For he is our peace, who hath made both one, and hath broken down the middle wall of partition between us; having abolished in his flesh the enmity, even the law of commandments contained in ordinances; for to make in himself of twain one new man, so making peace; and that he might reconcile both unto God in one body by the cross, having slain the enmity thereby: and came and preached peace to you which were afar off, and to them that were nigh. For through him we both have access by one Spirit unto the Father. (Ephesians 2:13-18)

Finally, to remind us that the idea that He wanted His followers to avenge His death was the very furthest thing from His mind, we read in Isaiah that He made intercession for sinners. Jesus' words from the cross were "Father, forgive them; for they know not what they do" (Luke 23:34).

CONCLUSION

What I have written above is by no means an exhaustive list of ways in which Isaiah 53 points to the death and resurrection of the Messiah Jesus. If Rashi is wrong about the passage being about Israel suffering on behalf of the Gentiles and if Rabbi Alshech is right that it is about the sufferings of the Messiah, is there any other candidate who can be found apart from Jesus who does fulfill it? The Suffering Servant of Isaiah is the Messiah who redeems His people from their sins. Isaiah of course is not a Gentile, but the great Jewish prophet to whom God revealed truths which were to be fulfilled centuries later in the person of Yeshua/Jesus the Messiah.

For the life of the flesh is in the blood:

and I have given it to you upon the

altar to make an atonement for your

souls: for it is the blood that maketh

an atonement for the soul.

(Leviticus 17:11)

CHAPTER 8

"WHEN I SEE THE BLOOD"

———◆———

In the previous chapter, we looked at the verse in Isaiah 52 which says the Servant shall "sprinkle many nations" and related this to the blood of atonement provided by Jesus. In the New Testament book of Hebrews, the connection is made between the bloodshed in the animal sacrifices as required in Leviticus and the blood Jesus shed as the Messiah:

> For if the blood of bulls and of goats, and the ashes of an heifer sprinkling the unclean, sanctifieth to the purifying of the flesh: how much more shall the blood of Christ, who through the eternal Spirit offered himself without spot to God, purge your conscience from dead works to serve the living God? (Hebrews 9:13-14)

> For when Moses had spoken every precept to all the people according to the law, he took the blood of calves and of goats, with water, and scarlet wool, and hyssop, and sprinkled both the book, and all the people, saying, This is the blood of the testament which God hath enjoined unto you. Moreover he sprinkled with blood both the tabernacle, and all the vessels

of the ministry. And almost all things are by the law purged
with blood; and without shedding of blood is no remission.
(Hebrews 9:19-22)

In modern Judaism, there is no longer any place for the offering
of sacrifices to cover sin through the shedding of the blood of the
animal offered to the Lord. When the Temple was destroyed in 70
AD by the Romans, the place where the sacrifices should be offered
was taken away from the Jewish people. At that time, the Sanhedrin
reconvened under the leadership of Rabbi Yochanan ben Zakkai, who
established the academy at Yavneh where he set up a way to keep part
of the Torah without sacrifices, priesthood, and Temple. According
to the classic midrash in Avot D'Rabbi Nathan (4:5):

> The Temple is destroyed. We never witnessed its glory. But
> Rabbi Joshua did. And when he looked at the Temple ruins
> one day, he burst into tears. "Alas for us! The place which
> atoned for all the sins of the people of Israel lies in ruins!"

Then Rabbi Zakkai spoke to him these words of comfort:

> Be not grieved, my son. There is another way of gaining ritual
> atonement, even though the Temple is destroyed. We must
> gain ritual atonement through deeds of lovingkindness.

So he changed the way of gaining atonement from the ritual described in Leviticus 16-17 to "deeds of loving kindness." The Talmud
and later rabbis followed his lead in saying that atonement is now
provided by repentance without sacrifices, a teaching they based on
verses like these:

> To obey is better than sacrifice. (1 Samuel 15:22)

> To what purpose is the multitude of your sacrifices unto me?
> saith the LORD: I am full of the burnt offerings of rams, and
> the fat of fed beasts; and I delight not in the blood of bullocks,

or of lambs, or of he goats. . . . Bring no more vain oblations; incense is an abomination unto me. (Isaiah 1:11, 13)

For I desired mercy, and not sacrifice; and the knowledge of God more than burnt offerings. (Hosea 6:6)

Based on these and other Scriptures, Judaism developed a theology which relegated the sacrificial system to ancient history. The fact that the Temple no longer stood and, therefore, there was no access to the place appointed by God to offer the sacrifices seemed to confirm this view. Therefore, the Rabbis decreed that God was able to forgive sins through repentance, prayers, fasting, and good deeds, which replaced the blood of the animal sacrifices. In this, they were only developing ideas that had been around since the Babylonian exile and the development of the synagogue and the home as an alternative to Temple worship.

As long as the Temple stood the altar atoned for Israel. But now a man's table atones for him. [1]

Sincere repentance is considered enough to cover sin:

Whoever commits a transgression and is filled with shame thereby all his sins are forgiven him. [2]

Maimonides wrote that repentance atones for all sins:

At this time when the Temple no longer exists, and we have no atonement altar, nothing is left but repentance. Repentance atones for all transgressions. Even if a man was wicked throughout his life and repented at the end, we must not mention anything about his wickedness to him, as it is written, "And as for the wickedness of the wicked he will not stumble because of it in the day when he turns from his wickedness." (Ezekiel 33:12; Yom Kippur itself atones for those who repent as it is written, "For it is on this day that atonement shall be made for you."[3] (Leviticus 16:30)

So does God say that sacrifices are not needed to cover sins? Let us go back to the Bible verses from the Prophets quoted above and look at them in context. The issue God has with His people is that they are offering sacrifices without sincerity and continuing in sin at the same time. God is not actually saying, "You don't need to offer any sacrifices." What He is saying is, "Your sacrifices are meaningless because you are just going through the outward motions of pleasing me while your hearts and your actions are far from me." He is calling on them to repent *and* to offer the sacrifices from a true heart, not to repent *instead of* offering the sacrifices.

If we look at the whole teaching of the Bible, we find that almost everything involving a covenant between God and humanity is sanctified by an offering involving the shedding of blood. Adam and Eve put on fig leaves to cover their nakedness, but God did not accept this covering and clothed them in animal skins, involving the death of the animal (Genesis 3:7, 21). Cain offered the fruit of the ground and was not accepted, while Abel offered "the firstlings [firstborn]of his flock" (i.e., a sacrifice involving the death of an animal) and was accepted (Genesis 4:3-4). Noah offered a sacrifice of the clean animals that came out of the ark, and this was "a sweet savour" to the Lord (Genesis 8:20-22). God made the covenant with Abraham concerning his descendants and the Promised Land after Abraham had made the sacrifice of animals which God required of him (Genesis 15). After God gave the Torah, Moses read the commandments to the people and sprinkled the blood of the sacrificed animals on the people and on the altar to seal their covenant with God (Exodus 24:3-8).

Was this because God was bloodthirsty, or was it some primitive ritual which has now been done away with? Or was God making a serious point that needed to be understood? According to the Bible, death came into the world because of sin:

And unto Adam [God] said, Because thou hast hearkened
unto the voice of thy wife, and hast eaten of the tree, of which
I commanded thee, saying, Thou shalt not eat of it: cursed is
the ground for thy sake; in sorrow shalt thou eat of it all the
days of thy life; thorns also and thistles shall it bring forth to
thee; and thou shalt eat the herb of the field; in the sweat of
thy face shalt thou eat bread, till thou return unto the ground;
for out of it wast thou taken: for dust thou art, and unto dust
shalt thou return. (Genesis 3:17-19)

From the prophet Ezekiel, we read, "the soul that sinneth, it shall
die" (Ezekiel 18:4).

So in order to cover sin and escape from its penalty (death), there
needs to be another who dies in our place. Under the covenant with
Moses, this was the animal which sacrificed its blood (and therefore
died) in accordance with the commandments given in the Torah. This
was the only way in which the barrier between God and humanity,
caused by sin, could be removed. God is holy, and we are not, and the
only way we can relate to the Holy One is on His terms not ours. The
Lord makes it clear that He requires the shedding of blood in order for
us to come into relationship with Him. In Leviticus 17:11, we read:

For the life of the flesh is in the blood: and I have given it to
you upon the altar to make an atonement for your souls: for
it is the blood that maketh an atonement for the soul.

We also read of the importance of the blood in connection with
the night of the Passover when the people were instructed to sacrifice
a lamb and place the blood of the lamb on the doorposts of their
houses. The Angel of death would then pass over them:

For the LORD will pass through to smite the Egyptians; and
when he seeth the blood upon the lintel, and on the two side
posts, the LORD will pass over the door, and will not suffer
the destroyer to come in unto your houses to smite you.
(Exodus 12:23)

Since the destruction of the Temple, there has been no blood sacrifice, and modern Judaism no longer considers it necessary. Yet, according to the verse above from Leviticus, it is vital. I am not advocating, however, that Judaism returns to the sacrifice of animals, even if that were possible in the modern world because the final sacrifice for sin has been made once and for all by Jesus the Messiah, "the Lamb of God who takes away the sin of the world." He shed His blood at the time of the Passover, for the forgiveness of the sins of all mankind:

> But Christ being come an high priest of good things to come . . . by his own blood he entered in once into the holy place, having obtained eternal redemption for us. For if the blood of bulls and of goats, and the ashes of an heifer sprinkling the unclean, sanctifieth to the purifying of the flesh: how much more shall the blood of Christ, who through the eternal Spirit offered himself without spot to God, purge your conscience from dead works to serve the living God? (Hebrews 9:11-14)

Under the Old Covenant, the worshipper found forgiveness through repentance and faith in the blood of the sacrificed animal. He recognized that he deserved to die, but God in His mercy accepted this sacrifice in his place. The blood of the animal itself only had value in that it pointed forward to the blood of the Messiah, who was yet to come. Under the New Covenant, the same principle applies. We find forgiveness through repentance and faith in the blood of the Messiah shed for our sins:

> [B]ut now once in the end of the world hath [Christ] appeared to put away sin by the sacrifice of himself. And as it is appointed unto men once to die, but after this the judgment: so Christ was once offered to bear the sins of many; and unto them that look for him shall he appear the second time without sin unto salvation. (Hebrews 9:26-28)

So just as with the Old Covenant, it is still imperative that those who come to God must repent of their sins and put their trust in the sacrifice He has appointed. Under the Old Covenant, it was the blood of a sacrificed animal. Under the New Covenant, it is the one perfect sacrifice of the blood of Jesus the Messiah of which the sacrifices of the Old Testament foreshadowed of what was to come. Through accepting this sacrifice, we find our way to a covenant relationship with God.

Just before He was taken away to be crucified Jesus celebrated the Passover with His disciples. He then took the familiar symbols of matzo (unleavened) bread and wine which spoke of the Exodus from Egypt and reapplied them to Himself.

> And he said unto them, With desire I have desired to eat this passover with you before I suffer: for I say unto you, I will not any more eat thereof, until it be fulfilled in the kingdom of God. And he took the cup, and gave thanks, and said, Take this, and divide it among yourselves: for I say unto you, I will not drink of the fruit of the vine, until the kingdom of God shall come. And he took bread, and gave thanks, and brake it, and gave unto them, saying, This is my body which is given for you: this do in remembrance of me. Likewise also the cup after supper, saying, This cup is the new testament in my blood, which is shed for you. (Luke 22:15-20)

What He was saying is that there is now a greater Exodus offered, not just bringing people out of physical slavery in Egypt but bringing us out of slavery to sin and into the Promised Land of a relationship with God. In Exodus, God required the blood on the doorposts of the Israelite houses for the Angel of Death to pass over them and thus deliver them from death to life. Today, God requires the blood of the Messiah to be applied to our individual lives in order that we can pass from eternal death and separation from God into eternal life in the kingdom of God. In the Jewish Passover service, the cup taken after supper, the cup Jesus related to the New Covenant, is the third cup, which is known as the Cup of Redemption.

So God replaced the animal sacrifices with the sacrifice of the Messiah as our atonement for sin, rather than replacing them with prayer, good deeds, and fasting. As we shall see in the next chapter, there is also a vital link between the sacrificial death of the Messiah and the destruction of the Temple which caused the end of the animal sacrifices.

When Jesus died on the cross, His last words were, "It is finished!" (John 19:30). By this, He did not mean His life was finished but that the work of redemption was finished and there was nothing more needed to be added to it. This also meant that from that moment on, the animal sacrifices in the Temple became redundant and instead of being an act of faith and obedience to God, they became an act of unbelief and disobedience. The letter to the Hebrews in the New Testament is written to show Jewish believers in Jesus that they should not take part in animal sacrifices in the Temple because that would be like trampling underfoot the blood of the covenant sealed by Jesus' blood shed on the cross (Hebrews 10:26-39).

There is also an exact parallel to the Prophets speaking against the offering of insincere sacrifices in the verses quoted at the beginning of this chapter to be found in the New Testament. As we have seen, the issue was not that God did not want sacrifices. It was that the sacrifices offered without repentance and faith and without deeds of righteousness were meaningless and an offence to God.

In 1 Corinthians 11:27-29, Paul writes:

> Wherefore whosoever shall eat this bread, and drink this cup of the Lord, unworthily, shall be guilty of the body and blood of the Lord. But let a man examine himself, and so let him eat of that bread, and drink of that cup. For he that eateth and drinketh unworthily, eateth and drinketh damnation to himself, not discerning the Lord's body.

This means that for people to take the bread and the wine in remembrance of the Lord Jesus "in an unworthy manner" is not acceptable to God. What God is looking for is genuine repentance and faith in Jesus as Savior and Lord. If that is lacking, then taking the bread and the wine is exactly the same as offering the sacrifices without repentance, the issue for which the Lord was condemning Israel in the passage from Isaiah quoted at the beginning of this chapter. Far from doing us good, this practice actually brings us under the judgment of God.

Therefore, the teaching of the New Testament is entirely consistent with the Tenach on this issue where the blood of the Old Covenant was a foreshadowing of the shed blood of the Messiah to come. God requires the blood of atonement, but also that the people receive the atoning sacrifice in a worthy manner, with faith and repentance operating in their hearts. Under the Tenach, the blood of atonement was provided by the animal sacrifices. Under the New Testament, it is provided by the sacrifice of the Messiah, which is the better and eternal covenant by which God now puts Jews and Gentiles right with Himself.

Back in Genesis 14:18-20, we read of a mysterious person who in some way prefigures all of this. He is called Melchizedek (which means King of Righteousness) and is King of Salem (King of Peace). He meets Abraham, who is on his way back from the first war recorded in the Bible. Coming back from a war is a good time to meet the King of Righteousness and Peace. Melchizedek offers Abraham bread and wine, just as Jesus offers bread and wine to His disciples as a symbol of His body and blood sacrificed for the sins of the world (Luke 22:19-20).

So who was Melchizedek? An appearance of the Messiah to Abraham, or a type of the Messiah? It is not clear from the text, but it is certain that he was a highly exalted person. In Psalm 110, we have a prophecy of someone who will be "a priest for ever after the order of Melchizedek." Who could this be? To make this question even more intriguing, Psalm 110 begins with the words, "The LORD said unto my Lord." So how can the Lord speak to the Lord? Only if God is a plural unity, the issue we have looked at already in Chapter 5.

The New Testament Letter to the Hebrews describes Melchizedek as "priest of the most high God" . . . "without father, without mother, without descent, having neither beginning of days, nor end of life; but made like unto the Son of God; abideth a priest continually" (Hebrews 7:1 –3). It goes on to say how a better covenant is now in place, which replaces the sacrificial system mediated by the Levitical Priests, who needed to offer animal sacrifices over and over again. This covenant is mediated once and for all through the sacrifice of Jesus the Messiah and never needs to be replaced. All who enter into it through repentance and faith in Him need no longer fear the judgment of God:

> And as it is appointed unto men once to die, but after this the judgment: so Christ was once offered to bear the sins of many; and unto them that look for him shall he appear the second time without sin unto salvation. (Hebrews 9:27-28)

CHAPTER 9

THE FALL OF THE SECOND TEMPLE

———————◆———————

So what about the animal sacrifices today? There are some Orthodox Jews in Jerusalem who wish to rebuild the Temple and bring in the animal sacrifices again. The Temple Mount Faithful have set up their reconstituted Sanhedrin and are recreating the items used in the Temple and preparing priests to recreate the sacrificial system. According to their website:

> The goal of the Temple Mount and Land of Israel Faithful Movement is the building of the Third Temple on the Temple Mount in Jerusalem in our lifetime in accordance with the Word of G-d and all the Hebrew prophets and the liberation of the Temple Mount from Arab (Islamic) occupation so that it may be consecrated to the Name of G-d.[1]

Once they have done this, they believe Messiah, son of David, will arrive.

This is a minority concern, however, encouraged by some Christians who for prophetic reasons want to see a rebuilt Temple. One problem is that the Temple area is under Islamic control at present, and any attempt to rebuild the Temple where the Dome of the Rock mosque now stands would cause an uproar in the Islamic world. Apart from this there are massive problems about any reconstituting of the sacrificial system, which involves setting up the Priesthood and the Sanhedrin again. As a Jewish friend once said to me, "We've got enough problems agreeing on a Chief Rabbi. You want us to agree on who should be High Priest!" Jewish opponents of the Temple reconstruction project say it would mean the end of both Judaism and Zionism.[2]

The destruction of the Second Temple was an event of enormous significance for the Jewish people: Rabbi Ken Spiro writes:

> The destruction of the Second Temple is one of the most important events in the history of the Jewish people, and certainly one of the most depressing. It is a sign that God has withdrawn from (though certainly not abandoned) the Jews. Although the Jews will survive in accordance with the promise that they will be an "eternal nation," the special relationship with God they enjoyed while the Temple stood is gone . . . Why was the Second Temple destroyed? Because of sinat chinam, causeless hatred of one Jew for another (Talmud—Yomah).[3]

There has to be a reason why God permitted this calamity to happen to Israel. Rabbi Spiro is right that the destruction of the Temple is one of the most important events in the history of the Jewish people. But the answer given in the Talmud is not satisfactory. As the Rabbi says, the Jewish people today are not in the same relationship with God which they enjoyed in earlier days when they experienced extensive divine protection and victory over their enemies under such leaders as Moses, Joshua, Gideon and David. Rather they have experienced the fulfillment of Deuteronomy 28:64-66:

> And the LORD shall scatter thee among all people, from the one end of the earth even unto the other; and there thou shalt serve other gods, which neither thou nor thy fathers have known, even wood and stone. And among these nations shalt

thou find no ease, neither shall the sole of thy foot have rest: but the LORD shall give thee there a trembling heart, and failing of eyes, and sorrow of mind: and thy life shall hang in doubt before thee; and thou shalt fear day and night, and shalt have none assurance of thy life.

Why is this? A reading of the whole of Deuteronomy 28 gives a very clear answer. Verses 1-14 record all the blessings of God's peace, prosperity and protection given to Israel on one simple condition: "if thou shalt hearken diligently unto the voice of the LORD thy God, to observe and to do all his commandments" (vs. 1). The remainder of the chapter (verses 15-68) records God's judgments on Israel if they disobey. The whole history of Israel recorded in the Bible can be seen as the outworking of this chapter in the direct experience of the people of Israel. When the people turned away from God, they experienced His judgments in terms of foreign invasion, drought, social disintegration, and confusion. At these times, God raised up prophets and leaders who spoke His message and showed the people the way back to God's blessing as when He led them to victory over foreign invaders and back to peace. But when they refused to listen, He allowed the Gentile nations to punish them.

As Rabbi Spiro says, by far the greatest suffering in Israel's history began with the destruction of the Temple in Jerusalem by the Romans and the beginning of the dispersion. Could it be coincidental this happened just one generation after God spoke through Yeshua, Jesus of Nazareth, not only through His words, but also through His death and resurrection? God spoke to Moses and said:

I will raise them up a Prophet from among their brethren, like unto thee, and will put my words in his mouth; and he shall speak unto them all that I shall command him. And it shall come to pass, that whosoever will not hearken unto my words which he shall speak in my name, I will require it of him. (Deuteronomy 18:18-19)

If Jesus was that Prophet whom Moses was pointing to, we have an explanation for the fall of the Temple in 70 AD which makes much more sense than the reason given in the Talmud. The people, especially the religious leadership, did not give heed to Jesus' words, and so God allowed this calamity to happen. This is a much more plausible reason than the "causeless hatred" theory. If causeless hatred was so serious that it was going to lead to the destruction of the Temple and the scattering of the Jewish people into the nations, surely God would have sent a prophet beforehand to tell people to love each other. In fact, He did. Jesus said:

> A new commandment I give unto you, That ye love one another; as I have loved you, that ye also love one another. (John 13:34)

If we look at the fall of the first Temple at the hands of the Babylonians, we find that God sent prophet after prophet to warn of the coming event. Jeremiah was the main prophet whom God raised up to speak to the generation before the fall of the Temple and the deportation of the Jewish people to Babylon. As a prophet He did three main things:

1. He told them what was going to happen.

2. He gave a reason for it.

3. He gave a promise of restoration.

For forty years, Jeremiah warned his generation that the Babylonians were going to invade and destroy Jerusalem and the Temple and take them into captivity unless they repented of their sins. The reason why it was going to happen was the worship of idols and the breaking of God's commandments:

> Behold, ye trust in lying words, that cannot profit. Will ye steal, murder, and commit adultery, and swear falsely, and burn incense unto Baal, and walk after other gods whom

ye know not; and come and stand before me in this house, which is called by my name, and say, We are delivered to do all these abominations? (Jeremiah 7:8-10)

Far from repenting, they mocked Jeremiah and rejected his message in preference of the false prophets who said they were going to have peace and safety. But Jeremiah was not just a prophet of doom. He also promised a return from Babylon and a hope for the future:

> For thus saith the LORD, That after seventy years be accomplished at Babylon I will visit you, and perform my good word toward you, in causing you to return to this place. For I know the thoughts that I think toward you, saith the LORD, thoughts of peace, and not of evil, to give you an expected end. (Jeremiah 29:10-11)

This promise was fulfilled when the Persians overthrew the Babylonian Empire and the Persian Emperor Cyrus issued a decree that the Jewish people should return to the Promised Land and rebuild the Temple in Jerusalem (Ezra 1:1-4). In this way, the covenant was being fulfilled as the descendants of Abraham returned to the land God promised to Abraham.

Jeremiah also looked beyond the return of the Jewish people to a time when God would make a new covenant with the house of Israel. The terms of this covenant would be different from the covenant God made with Israel when He brought them out of Egypt:

> [T]his shall be the covenant that I will make with the house of Israel; After those days, saith the LORD, I will put my law in their inward parts, and write it in their hearts; and will be their God, and they shall be my people. And they shall teach no more every man his neighbour, and every man his brother, saying, Know the LORD: for they shall all know me, from the least of them unto the greatest of them, saith the LORD: for I will forgive their iniquity, and I will remember their sin no more. (Jeremiah 31:33-34)

The New Covenant points to the Messiah who was to come to deal with the problem of the sin nature, which causes us all to break God's commandments. When Jesus came in fulfillment of Isaiah 53 (and many other prophecies), He brought in the New Covenant through dying as a sacrifice for the sins of the world at the time of the Passover. At the time that the Jewish people were offering the Passover lambs to remember the blood of the lamb that protected them from the Angel of Death (see Exodus 12), Jesus was put to death by crucifixion in fulfillment of Psalm 22, Daniel 9:26 and Zechariah 12:10. He was the "Lamb of God, which taketh away the sin of the world" (John 1:29). As we have seen in the previous chapter, He saves from eternal death all those who come under the protection of His blood.

Did the coming of the New Covenant mean that God was finished with the Jewish people and that the covenant made with Abraham no longer applied? Much of the church actually teaches this in so called "replacement theology," which means that the promises to Israel are now given to the church. But it is significant that after God gave His promise of the New Covenant, He said that as long as the sun, the moon, and the stars exist, so long will Israel be a nation before the Lord (Jeremiah 31:35-36).

If we look carefully at Jesus' words, we discover that in relation to Israel, Jesus, too, functioned in the same prophetic way that Jeremiah did:

1. He warned of the coming catastrophe.

2. He gave a reason for it.

3. He gave a promise of restoration.

As Jesus was riding into Jerusalem at the beginning of the week that would lead up to His crucifixion and resurrection, He stopped halfway down the Mount of Olives and wept over the city and said:

> If thou hadst known, even thou, at least in this thy day, the things which belong unto thy peace! but now they are hid from thine eyes. For the days shall come upon thee, that

> thine enemies shall cast a trench about thee, and compass
> thee round, and keep thee in on every side, and shall lay thee
> even with the ground, and thy children within thee; and they
> shall not leave in thee one stone upon another; because thou
> knewest not the time of thy visitation. (Luke 19:42-44)

Jesus prophesied the destruction of Jerusalem and the Temple by the Romans that happened in 70 AD. He told those who believed in Him to flee from the city when they saw the armies gathering because this was going to lead to a time of terrible slaughter and destruction. He also knew that the motivation of the Jewish revolt would be a false Messianic hope in a coming deliverer from the Romans. This happened in the second Jewish revolt (132-135 AD), led by Bar Cochba, who was proclaimed the Messiah by Rabbi Akiba:

> [F]or there shall be great distress in the land, and wrath upon
> this people. And they shall fall by the edge of the sword,
> and shall be led away captive into all nations: and Jerusalem
> shall be trodden down of the Gentiles, until the times of the
> Gentiles be fulfilled. (Luke 21:23-24)

In these verses, Jesus warned of the coming destruction of Jerusalem, and the dispersion of the Jewish people into the lands of the Gentiles. He also gave a reason for it—"because thou knewest not the time of the visitation" (Luke 19:44). In other words, the dispersion happened because Jesus was not recognized as the Messiah. In this sense, there is a certain truth in the "causeless hatred" theory of Judaism, but not as it is understood today. The question has to be asked, "Who is the object of the causeless hatred?" Today the Jewish answer to this is that "causeless hatred" meant the hostility of different Jewish factions defending Jerusalem that allowed the Romans to break through and take the city. But Jesus spoke about His coming rejection and crucifixion and used exactly this phrase to describe the opposition to Himself:

He that hateth me hateth my Father also. If I had not done among them the works which none other man did, they had not had sin: but now have they both seen and hated both me and my Father. But this cometh to pass, that the word might be fulfilled that is written in their law, *They hated me without a cause.* (John 15:23-25, quoting Psalm 69:4; emphasis added)

It is fascinating to note there is a warning of coming destruction of the Temple in the Talmud. Although this is generally the last place one would look to find some indication that Jesus is the Messiah, there is a passage that implies something happened forty years before the destruction of the Temple pointing to its coming destruction and even to the fact that it had become spiritually desolate forty years before it became physically desolate. It was forty years before its destruction that Jesus gave His prophecy of its coming destruction and gave Himself as a sacrifice for the sins of the world, so doing away with the need for animal sacrifices.

At the time of the Second Temple, the practice on Yom Kippur, the Day of Atonement, was to take two goats and sacrifice them to the Lord according to Leviticus 16. The first goat was "for the LORD" and the second goat was "l'azazel" for the scapegoat. The High Priest would choose the goats by lots, and it was considered a good omen if he brought out the goat "for the LORD" with his right hand and a bad omen if he brought it out with his left hand. The blood of the first goat was taken into the Holy of Holies, and the second goat was sent out into the wilderness, after having the sins of the people placed upon it in accordance with Leviticus 16:21. A scarlet sash was tied around the neck of the scapegoat, and it was then taken to a precipice in the wilderness about twelve miles from Jerusalem. In their book *The Fall Feasts of Israel*, Mitch and Zhava Glaser describe what happened next:

When the goat finally arrived at the precipice, the attending priest removed the red sash from its head and divided it, returning half to the animal's horns and tying the other half to a protrusion on the cliff. He then pushed the animal backwards over the cliff to its death.

In connection with this ceremony an interesting tradition arose, which is mentioned in the Mishna. A portion of the crimson sash was attached to the door of the Temple before the goat was sent into the wilderness. The sash would turn from red to white as the goat met its end, signaling to the people that God had accepted their sacrifice and their sins were forgiven. This was based on the verse in Isaiah where the prophet declared: "Come now, and let us reason together," says the Lord, "though your sins are as scarlet, they shall be as white as snow; though they are red like crimson, they will be like wool" (Isaiah 1:18). The Mishna tells us that forty years before the destruction of the Temple, the sash stopped turning white. That of course was approximately the year that Christ died.[4]

In fact, there are four signs recorded in the Talmud (Yoma 39a, b) of events that happened during this forty-year period before the destruction of the Temple:

1. The lot for the Lord's goat did not come up in the right hand of the high priest.

2. The scarlet cord tied to the door of the Temple on the Day of Atonement stopped turning white after the scapegoat had been cast over the precipice.

3. The westernmost light on the Temple candelabra would not burn. It is believed that this light was used to light the other lights of the candelabra.

4. The Temple doors would open by themselves. The rabbis saw this as an ominous fulfillment of Zechariah 11:1, "Open thy doors, O Lebanon, that fire may devour thy cedars." The opening of the doors to let in the consuming fire foretold the destruction of the Temple itself by fire.[5]

The fact that two of these signs relate to the sacrifices on the Day of Atonement and that all of them took place over the forty-year period before the destruction of the Second Temple cannot be a coincidence. It points to the real reason why God permitted its destruction, and that has to do with the rejection of the Messiah by the Sanhedrin and the continuation of animal sacrifices after the one final and perfect sacrifice for sin had been offered. Once Jesus had offered Himself as a sacrifice for sin and atonement, God never again accepted the animal sacrifices offered on Yom Kippur. This explains why during the forty years before the destruction of the Temple, the sash never turned white and the goat for the Lord was always taken with the left hand (statistically this is virtually impossible).

Apart from this passage in the Talmud, there is one major prophecy in the Tenach that shows the Messiah will come before the destruction of the second Temple and points to the reason for its desolation. In Daniel 9, we are told of the encounter Daniel had with the angel Gabriel, when he prayed for the restoration of the Temple in Jerusalem after the seventy years of desolation prophesied by Jeremiah had been fulfilled. He is given a detailed prophecy (the famous "70 weeks of years") which speaks of the rebuilding of Jerusalem "in troublesome times" and the eventual destruction of the city and the sanctuary (the Temple). Before that happens, "Messiah shall be cut off":

> And after threescore and two weeks shall Messiah be cut off, but not for himself: and the people of the prince that shall come shall destroy the city and the sanctuary; and the end thereof shall be with a flood, and unto the end of the war desolations are determined. (Daniel 9:26)

A young man named Rachmiel Frydland had studied at a Yeshiva in Warsaw before World War II began. Some Christians showed him this passage from Daniel which troubled him deeply. He searched for the Jewish answer to their claim that the verse was about Jesus and had some difficulty finding any material about it, as study of the book of Daniel is discouraged because of the information it contains about the Messiah. Eventually, he found some commentaries that followed the teaching of Rashi who said that the one referred to here is King Agrippa who died just before the destruction of the Second Temple. He concluded that if the best the rabbis can do is to say this verse is fulfilled by an obscure Gentile king, they must have got it wrong. The only person who could possibly have fulfilled this verse is someone who came as Messiah, was cut off, dying a violent death, not for himself but for the sins of others at some time before the Romans came and destroyed the city (Jerusalem) and the sanctuary (the Temple)—Jesus the Messiah. The story of Rachmiel Frydland's faith in the Messiah and his miraculous survival of the Holocaust in Poland is written in his book *When Being Jewish Was a Crime.*[6]

Jesus also prophesied the coming destruction of Jerusalem and the Temple followed by words of a hopeful future when this desolation will be reversed (as explained below). He said, "your house [the Temple] is left unto you desolate" (Matthew 23:38). The Temple was left desolate in a spiritual sense immediately after the death and resurrection of Jesus, for the reasons given above. From that point on, God no longer accepted the sacrifices offered in the Temple that became spiritually desolate. Forty years later, physical desolation also came to the building as the Romans destroyed it in fulfillment of the words of Daniel 9:26 and of Luke 19:41-44.

But that is not the end of the story. Speaking prophetically to Jerusalem, Jesus went on to look forward to the day of redemption, saying

> For I say unto you [i.e., Jerusalem], Ye shall not see me henceforth, till ye shall say, Blessed is he that cometh in the name of the Lord. (Matthew 23:39)

This is not just any old phrase. In Hebrew, it is "Baruch ha ba be shem adonai."

This is the traditional greeting for the coming Messiah. Jesus is saying something is going to happen that will change the fortunes of the city whereby will no longer be "trodden down of [ruled by] the

Gentiles" (Luke 21:24). This lines up with the numerous prophecies in the Tenach of Jerusalem's coming redemption.

What will cause this change? It will be the recognition of Jesus as the Messiah and the resulting outpouring of the Holy Spirit on those who call on His name. This will be the trigger for His second coming to the Earth as the Jewish people welcome Him as Messiah with the words, "Blessed is he that cometh in the name of the Lord" (Matthew 23:39).

CHAPTER 10

NO PEACE—NO MESSIAH

In the prophecy of Daniel mentioned at the end of the previous chapter, it says that Messiah will come before the destruction of the second Temple and that following His coming there will be wars and desolations. This, of course, does not square with the majority view of Messiah in the Jewish community today. In discussion with a Jewish friend, he said to me, "Your Jesus can't be the Messiah because there is no peace in the world."

I told him that Jesus came the first time to save us from our sins in fulfillment of the prophecies in the Bible of the Suffering Servant and that He is coming again to judge the world in righteousness and bring in the promised age of peace and justice.

"Where did you get this idea of a 'second coming' from? Was it because Jesus did not succeed the first time that he's got to have another go? It doesn't say anything in the Bible about the Messiah coming twice."

Maybe he had been reading this in Rabbi Kaplan's book, *The Real Messiah?* which states:

> The main task of the Messiah was to bring the world back to God and to abolish all war, suffering and injustice from the

world. Clearly, Jesus did not accomplish this. In order to get around this failure on the part of Jesus, Christians invented the doctrine of the "Second Coming." All the prophecies that Jesus did not fulfil the first time are supposed to be taken care of the second time around. However the Jewish Bible offers absolutely no evidence to support the Christian doctrine of a "Second Coming."[1]

He may also have read the "Operation Judaism Fact Pack" compiled by Rabbi S. Arkush, designed to give the answer to Christian claims of Jesus being the Messiah. This is what he says the Messiah will do when He comes:

1. Messiah will bring universal peace. (Isaiah 2:4)

2. Families will live together in perfect harmony. (Malachi 3:24)

3. Even the animals will live together in peace. (Isaiah 11:6)

4. There will be no more illness. (Isaiah 35:5-6)

5. There will be no more sorrow. (Isaiah 65:19)

6. There will be no more death. (Isaiah 25:8)

7. The exiled of Israel will return to their land. (Ezekiel 39:25-28)

8. The ten lost tribes will also return. (Isaiah 27:13)

9. Even the dead will rise up and return. (Ezekiel 37:12)

10. The nations will be gathered for judgment. (Joel 3:2)

11. No sin will be found in Israel. (Jeremiah 50:20)

12. The cities of Israel will be rebuilt with precious stones. (Isaiah 54:11-12)

13. Even Sodom will be rebuilt. (Ezekiel 16:55)

14. The Divine Presence will dwell among Israel. (Ezekiel 37:27-28)

15. Joy and peace will reign in Jerusalem. (Isaiah 65:18-23)

16. All Israel will keep the Law. (Ezekiel 36:27)

17. Sacrifices will again be offered in the Temple. (Malachi 3:3-4)

18. There will be no more idolatry. (Isaiah 2:18)

19. All nations will be united under one rule. (Daniel 2:44)

20. There will be only one faith, and all nations will worship the God of Israel. (Isaiah 66:23)[2]

Clearly, there has not been universal peace since Jesus came, and if you put the average lion in a cage with the average lamb, there will not be a very bright future for the lamb. So does this mean Jesus is not the Messiah prophesied in the Bible?

A PROBLEM FOR RABBINIC JUDAISM

Before we go on to consider the answer to this, we have to say that the Rabbis, too, have a problem over this issue. Even if we accept that all twenty passages listed above as Messianic prophecies, this list is far from complete. While the prophets did give a clear picture of the Messiah reigning with power on the earth while bringing about the redemption of Israel, the end of war, and universal knowledge of God (Isaiah 2:1-4, Isaiah 11:1-9, Ezekiel 40-48, Daniel 2:44, Zechariah 14), there is another set of prophecies that speak of the Messiah suffering as an atonement for sin; I have already referred to these in this book (Psalm 22, Isaiah 52:13-53.12, Daniel 9:25-26, Zechariah 12:10). It would seem that Rabbi Arkush would like to delete this portrait of Messiah altogether, but this has not always been the case.

As we have already seen in chapter seven, Alshech, the Chief Rabbi of Safed, Upper Galilee, in the 16th century said of Isaiah 53:

Our Rabbis with one voice accept and affirm the opinion that the prophet is speaking of the king Messiah, and we shall ourselves also adhere to the same view.[3]

Commenting on Zechariah 12:10, where the prophet says Israel will "look upon me whom they have pierced," Rabbi Alshech writes:

For they shall lift up their eyes unto me in perfect repentance when they see him whom they have pierced, that is, *Messiah, the Son of Joseph*; for our Rabbis, of blessed memory, have said that He will take upon Himself all the guilt of Israel, and shall then be slain in the war to make an atonement in such a manner that it shall be accounted as if Israel had pierced him, for on account of their sin He has died; and, therefore, in order that it may be reckoned to them as a perfect atonement, they will repent, and look to the Blessed One, saying that there is none beside Him to forgive those that mourn on account of Him who died for their sin: this is the meaning of They shall look upon me.[4] (emphasis added)

That this passage (Zechariah 12:10) refers to the Messiah is admitted by Aben Ezra and Abarbanel, and also by Rashi in his commentary on the Talmud.

Rabbi Alshech's mention of "Messiah, the Son of Joseph" is a reference to the view held within Judaism that there are two Messiahs, one called Messiah son of Joseph who suffers and dies and one called Messiah son of David, who rules and reigns. On this subject, David Baron writes:

The doctrine or theory of two Messiahs, a Messiah ben Joseph, who should suffer and die, and the Messiah ben David, who shall reign in power and glory can be traced back to the third or fourth century AD, and very probably originated in the perplexity of the Talmudists at the apparently irreconcilable pictures of a suffering, and yet a glorious Messiah, which they found in the prophecies

[Scriptures]. Instead of finding the solution in two advents of the one person, they explained the different scriptures as referring to two different persons.[5]

The suffering Messiah is given the name "Son of Joseph" because he suffers rejection and humiliation like Joseph in Egypt (Genesis 37-41). The reigning Messiah is given the name "Son of David" because he reigns in triumph like King David.

In the Talmud, we read of the identity of the person in Zechariah's prophecy:

> What is the cause of mourning mentioned in the last cited verse (Zechariah 12:10). Rabbi Dosa and the Rabbis differ on this point. One explained, The cause is the slaying of the Messiah the son of Joseph, and the other explained, The cause is the slaying of the evil inclination. It is well according to him who explains that the cause is the slaying of Messiah the son of Joseph, since that well agrees with the Scriptural verse, "And they shall look upon me because they have thrust him through, and they shall mourn for him as one that mourns for his only son; but according to him who explains the cause to be the slaying of the Evil Inclination, is this an occasion for mourning? Is not this rather an occasion for rejoicing? Why then should they weep?[6]

The argument here is over whether the cause of mourning in Zechariah 12:10 is the slaying of the Messiah or the slaying of the evil inclination (a phrase used in Judaism to describe what is wrong in human beings). The rabbi concludes it must be the slaying of the Messiah because the slaying of the evil inclination is a cause for joy, not mourning. Taken together with the view expressed by Rabbi Alshech in which Messiah son of Joseph is killed to make atonement for the guilt of Israel, this shows that the Rabbis have interpreted Zechariah 12:10 to be about the death of the Messiah. Although this view is different from the New Testament concept of

Jesus as the atoning sacrifice, these quotations show a rabbinic view of a suffering Messiah who dies as a sacrifice for the guilt of Israel.

Another interesting quotation is to be found in the Talmud where we read:

> Rabbi Yehoshua ben Levi noted the apparent contradiction in the following two verses. It is written: "and behold one like a son of man (Moshiach/Messiah) comes with the clouds of heaven" (Daniel 7:13). But it also says: "Rejoice greatly, O daughter of Zion, shout, O daughter of Jerusalem. Behold, your king shall come to you, righteous and saviour is he, a pauper and riding on an ass" (Zechariah 9:9). The verses may be reconciled: If they are worthy, Moshiach will appear with the clouds. If not, he will be a pauper and ride on an ass.[7]

In other words, whether the Messiah appears in glory or in humiliation depends on the spiritual condition of the generation when he comes. Again this contradicts the view we are presenting, but it does point to the fact that Rabbinic Judaism has to try to explain the reason for two quite different portraits of the Messiah—one as a Suffering Servant and one as a Conquering King.

AN ALTERNATIVE VIEW

So, are there two Messiahs? Does it depend on the spiritual state of the generation when Messiah appears as to whether he comes in humility or triumph?

Or do the prophets describe the same Messiah who is coming on two different occasions with two different aims? Let us now examine this view.

The Gospel account in the New Testament is obviously mainly concerned with things that happened during the life of Jesus and points to the conclusion that He is the Messiah fulfilling prophecy. The New Testament writers also teach that the same Jesus will come again in person at some unspecified date in the future. Therefore, we can conclude that the New Testament teaches two comings of the same Messiah. This is not just an incidental doctrine but is integral to the whole message of the New Testament. In addition to several passing references to the second coming in each Gospel, a whole section of each of the Synoptic Gospels is devoted to it (Matthew 24-25, Mark 13, Luke 21). John relates the purpose of this event in these words of Jesus as recorded in John's Gospel:

> And if I go and prepare a place for you, I will come again, and receive you unto myself; that where I am, there ye may be also. (John 14:3)

The hope of Messiah's return was the subject of the preaching of the apostles (Acts 3:19-21, Acts 17:30-31) and was taught by all the writers of the Epistles: Paul in 1 Thessalonians 4:13-5,11; 2 Thessalonians 2; also in James 5:1-8; in 2 Peter 2-3; in 1 John 3:2; and in Jude 14-15. It is the subject of most of the book of Revelation. This, by no means an exhaustive list of references to the second coming in the New Testament, shows that this has been an integral part of the Christian faith from its origin. It is not some new-fangled idea cooked up to explain to Jews how Jesus can be the Messiah while we live in a world where universal peace is far from being the condition. It has also been a historic doctrine of believing Christians throughout the Christian era, enshrined in the creeds of all major denominations and something Christians are told to remember every time they take the Lord's Supper or communion, when they are to remember the death of Jesus *until He comes again.*

MESSIAH'S REIGN BEGINS WITH JUDGMENT

Of course, if you don't believe the New Testament is inspired by God, the fact that it teaches that Jesus comes twice does not cut much ice. The question now has to be asked, "Do the Messianic prophecies in the Tenach (Old Testament) speak of two comings of the Messiah?"

One interesting fact which emerges when we study the Messianic prophecies referred to by Rabbi Arkush is that the important ones all have to do with God's judgment of mankind. Isaiah 2:1-4, with its glorious vision of the word of the Lord going forth from Jerusalem and universal peace resulting from this is followed by a passage dealing with the Lord's judgment on human arrogance and idolatry:

> For the day of the LORD of hosts shall be upon [against] every one that is proud and lofty, and upon every one that is lifted up . . .

> And the loftiness of man shall be bowed down, and the haughtiness of men shall be made low: and the LORD alone shall be exalted in that day. And the idols he shall utterly abolish. And they shall go into the holes of the rocks, and into the caves of the earth, for fear of the LORD, and for the glory of his majesty, when he ariseth to shake terribly the earth. In that day a man shall cast his idols of silver, and his idols of gold, which they made each one for himself to worship, to the moles and to the bats; to go into the clefts of the rocks, and into the tops of the ragged rocks, for fear of the LORD, and for the glory of his majesty, when he ariseth to shake terribly the earth. (Isaiah 2:12, 17-21)

The picture of the wicked hiding from the presence of the Lord "in the dens and in the rocks of the mountains" is also to be found in Revelation 6:15-17, describing what will happen before the second coming of Jesus.

In Isaiah 11, the one who will cause the wolf to dwell with the lamb and the Earth to be full of the knowledge of the Lord will also enter into judgment with humanity:

> [H]e shall not judge after the sight of his eyes, neither reprove after the hearing of his ears: but with righteousness shall he judge the poor, and reprove with equity for the meek of the earth: and he shall smite the earth with the rod of

his mouth, and with the breath of his lips shall he slay the wicked. (Isaiah 11:3-4)

The verse spoken of by Rabbi Arkush in Joel clearly speaks of the nations being gathered for judgment:

I will also gather all nations, and will bring them down into the valley of Jehoshaphat, and will plead with them there for my people and for my heritage Israel, whom they have scattered among the nations, and parted my land. (Joel 3:2)

Ezekiel 20:33-38 teaches that Israel, too, will have to submit to judgment before being allowed into the Messianic kingdom:

As I live, saith the Lord God, surely with a mighty hand, and with a stretched out arm, and with fury poured out, will I rule over you: and I will bring you out from the people, and will gather you out of the countries wherein ye are scattered, with a mighty hand, and with a stretched out arm, and with fury poured out. And I will bring you into the wilderness of the people, and there will I plead with you face to face. Like as I pleaded with your fathers in the wilderness of the land of Egypt, so will I plead with you, saith the Lord God. And I will cause you to pass under the rod, and I will bring you into the bond of the covenant: and I will purge out from among you the rebels, and them that transgress against me: I will bring them forth out of the country where they sojourn, and they shall not enter into the land of Israel: and ye shall know that I am the LORD.

In this, the Prophets are in perfect harmony with the Gospel where Jesus taught that the nations will be gathered for judgment at His second coming:

When the Son of man shall come in his glory, and all the holy angels with him, then shall he sit upon the throne of his glory: and before him shall be gathered all nations: and he shall separate them one from another, as a shepherd divideth his sheep from the goats: and he shall set the sheep on his right hand, but the goats on the left. (Matthew 25:31-33)

HOW WILL HUMANITY BE JUDGED?

There is a unity of belief between the Old and New Testaments on the necessity of judgment preceding the age of peace and justice in which the nations will be united under the rule of the Messiah, so the question now has to be asked: "On what basis will this judgment be made?"

Most of modern Judaism teaches that "the righteous of all nations have a place in the world to come" and that you should do your best to keep whatever religion you are born into. The Rabbis teach that God requires the Jews to keep the 613 commandments which are derived from the Torah and the Gentiles to keep the 7 Laws of Noah. A leaflet put out by the Lubavitch organization states that "These seven laws provide a basic minimum for the maintenance of moral civilization." They are:

1. Do not worship idols.

2. Do not blaspheme.

3. Do not murder.

4. Do not steal.

5. Do not commit immoral sexual acts.

6. Do not be cruel to animals.

7. Maintain justice.[8]

The problem about these laws is that most Jews I have spoken to as well as all Gentiles, except a handful who have specifically studied this subject, are totally ignorant of their existence, which makes it difficult to see how people can be judged on this basis. To say on this basis that you should keep whatever religion you were born into also raises some problems. While most religions do condemn murder, theft and sexual immorality, a number of major world religions (Roman Catholicism, Hinduism, Buddhism) allow practices which the Bible would consider idolatrous. Cruelty to animals is not a big deal in Islam as any visitor to the Middle East will soon discover. So in practice, it is hard to see how the so-called 7 Laws of Noah can be a basis for judging humanity, especially as most people have never heard of them.

I have never met any Jewish person who feels under any obligation to tell Gentiles that they should keep the 7 Laws of Noah. In practice, Judaism teaches the kind of universalism which is in keeping with the general trend in interfaith religious circles today. Writing in the Jewish journal *L'Eylah,* Rabbi Arye Forta contrasts this way of thinking with the Christian belief in one way of salvation through Jesus Christ:

> Judaism is not evangelical, but not out of insularity or parochialism. Judaism does not actively proselytise because it does not see the need to do so. "The righteous of all nations have a share in the world to come," said the Rabbis. The Jew can say to mankind, "You don't have to be Jewish to enter into a relationship with God; you just have to live a righteous life." Judaism defines righteousness in terms of the 7 laws of Noah and sees these as the basis of a moral and spiritual life.[9]

If the Rabbi is correct in saying "You just have to live a righteous life" to have a share in the world to come, then Heaven is going to be a very empty place because the Bible shows that even the best of us fail to live a completely righteous life. As we read in Ecclesiastes 7:20:

> [T]here is not a just man upon earth, that doeth good, and sinneth not.

Our attempts to make ourselves righteous are not good enough for God:

> But we are all as an unclean thing, and all our righteousnesses are as filthy rags. (Isaiah 64:6)

Paul agrees with this verdict and writes in Romans 3:10-12, quoting Psalm 14:1-3:

> There is none righteous, no, not one: there is none that understandeth, there is none that seeketh after God. They are all gone out of the way, they are together become unprofitable; there is none that doeth good, no, not one.

Paul goes on to show how it is through our identification with the righteousness of the Messiah who died as a sacrifice for our sins that we are made righteous and receive eternal life.

ARE ALL RELIGIONS ACCEPTABLE TO GOD?

Is this idea that all religions are acceptable to God in harmony with the teaching of the Prophets? What about ancient pagan religions involving witchcraft and human sacrifice still practiced in some places today and resurfacing in western nations? The Tenach teaches that the "gods of the nations are but idols" and contrasts the vanity of pagan worship (Isaiah 44:9-20) with the glory of the Lord, who is seen as the Redeemer to whom Israel is to bear witness to the nations:

Thus saith the LORD the King of Israel, and his redeemer the LORD of hosts; I am the first, and I am the last; and beside me there is no God. And who, as I, shall call, and shall declare it, and set it in order for me, since I appointed the ancient people? and the things that are coming, and shall come, let them shew unto them. Fear ye not, neither be afraid: have not I told thee from that time, and have declared it? ye are even my witnesses. (Isaiah 44:6-8)

According to Isaiah, salvation is offered not through the Babel of conflicting religious systems saying and doing things that contradict each other, but through the God of Israel:

Look unto me, and be ye saved, all the ends of the earth: for I am God, and there is none else. (Isaiah 45:22)

The God of Israel has a message for the whole of mankind:

I have sworn by myself, the word is gone out of my mouth in righteousness, and shall not return, That unto me every knee shall bow, every tongue shall swear. (Isaiah 45:23)

Is there any group of people seeking to make known this message to the whole of mankind today? Yes, the whole of the Bible has been translated into 405 languages, all the major languages of the world, the New Testament into 1034 languages, and portions of the Bible into a further 864 languages. Bible translators are working hard to translate the Bible into the remaining minority languages of the world. As a result, there are people all over the world who look to the God of Abraham, Isaac, and Jacob for salvation, which they have received through the Messiah to whom the Prophets bore witness before He came in the flesh. This has happened because of the faithful witness of the first Jewish disciples in Jesus who obeyed His command to go into the world and preach the Gospel (Matthew 28:18-20).

WORLD EVANGELISM AND THE SECOND COMING

What does this have to do with the first and second coming of the Messiah? A great deal. The New Testament belief is that the Messiah came the first time to bear the sins of the world and to offer Himself as the atoning sacrifice for all mankind. Through Him, both Jews and Gentiles may partake of the promises given by God to Israel and be reconciled to God (Ephesians 2:11-18) and join the believing church. In the original Greek of the New Testament, the word for church, *ekklesia,* means "the called out ones"—in other words, people who have been called out of the world to believe in Jesus as Messiah. It never means a building or a religious organization. It always means a group of people. The purpose of the true church in this age is to take the Gospel to the ends of the earth as Jesus told them to before He departed into heaven:

> All power is given unto me in heaven and in earth. Go ye therefore, and teach all nations, baptizing them in the name of the Father, and of the Son, and of the Holy Ghost: teaching them to observe all things whatsoever I have commanded you: and, lo, I am with you alway, even unto the end of the world. (Matthew 28:18-20)

This does not mean that all will receive it. The conditions of tribulation prophesied by Jesus for the end of this age make it clear that the majority will reject it. Jesus taught that this message will bring division between those who accept it and those who reject it:

> And this is the condemnation, that light is come into the world, and men loved darkness rather than light, because their deeds were evil. For every one that doeth evil hateth the light, neither cometh to the light, lest his deeds should be reproved. But he that doeth truth cometh to the light, that his deeds may be made manifest, that they are wrought in God. (John 3:19-21)

Those who do accept the Lord through coming to the point of genuine repentance and faith in Him experience the "new birth" which Jesus spoke about to Nicodemus:

Verily, verily, I say unto thee, Except a man be born again, he cannot see the kingdom of God. (John 3:3)

As a result of this new birth, the believer receives the Holy Spirit who begins the process of sanctification, reproducing in us the character of the Lord:

[T]he fruit of the Spirit is love, joy, peace, longsuffering, gentleness, goodness, faith. (Galatians 5:22)

Since the whole process is voluntary, the extent to which we show the character of the Holy Spirit depends on the extent to which we submit our lives to Him. It also needs to be pointed out that multitudes who profess to be Christians have never experienced this "new birth" and are therefore not Christians at all in the true sense and do not represent the true church.

This age will come to an end at the second coming of Jesus Christ when He will judge mankind on the basis of how we have responded to His offer of salvation. As we have said, this offer of salvation must first be given to all nations, which is now being done by the evangelistic work of the believing church. The rejection of this offer by the majority will lead to days of tribulation that will bring this age to a close as Jesus told His disciples when they asked Him, "What will be the sign of your coming and the close of the age?" His answer told of wars, famines, earthquakes, plagues, persecutions, and deception and that the age would end with "great tribulation, such as was not since the beginning of the world to this time, no, nor ever shall be" (Matthew 24:21). This again is in perfect harmony with the words of the Prophets who also taught there will be tribulation in the end of times:

And at that time shall Michael stand up, the great prince
which standeth for the children of thy people: and there
shall be a time of trouble, such as never was since there was
a nation even to that same time: and at that time thy people
shall be delivered, every one that shall be found written in
the book. (Daniel 12:1; see also Isaiah 24, Jeremiah 30,
Ezekiel 38-39, Zechariah 12-14)

THE TIME SPAN BETWEEN THE TWO
COMINGS OF THE MESSIAH

Although the Prophets did not make it clear there would be a
long time span between the first and second coming of the
Messiah, there is no reason why this should not be the correct interpretation of the "two Messiahs" problem. It also makes sense for
God to work it out this way as it involves us in making a free-will
choice and taking responsibility for our eternal destiny.

God could have sent the Redeemer immediately after the entry
of sin into the world in Genesis 3 if He had chosen to. Indeed, Eve's
response to the delivery of her first born child, "I have gotten a man
from the LORD" (Genesis 4:1) suggests she may have mistakenly
believed Cain to be the promised "seed of the woman" who would
bruise the serpent's head. The Targum of Palestine paraphrases this
verse: "And Adam knew his wife and she conceived and brought forth
Cain, and she said; 'I have obtained the man, the Angel of the Lord.'
This hope was dashed when Cain killed his brother Abel, but when
Eve later bore Seth, she exclaimed, "For God . . . hath appointed
me another seed instead of Abel, whom Cain slew" (Genesis 4:25).
The rabbis comment on this as follows, "[Eve] hinted at that seed
which would arise from another source . . . the king Messiah."[10]

The disciples of Jesus were also impatient for an immediate res-
olution of God's plan for the redemption of Israel when they asked
Jesus after the resurrection, "wilt thou at this time restore again
the kingdom to Israel?" (Acts 1:6). They understood that Jesus had

fulfilled the role of the suffering Messiah. They now looked to Him to fulfill immediately the role of reigning Messiah, bringing national redemption to Israel and peace to the world in fulfillment of Isaiah 2:1-4. Jesus' reply shows He did not rule out the ultimate goal of establishing the Messianic kingdom as foretold by the Prophets but that the immediate priority for them and for all true followers of Jesus Christ in this age is to spread the message of the Gospel:

> But ye shall receive power, after that the Holy Ghost is come upon you: and ye shall be witnesses unto me both in Jerusalem, and in all Judæa, and in Samaria, and unto the uttermost part of the earth. (Acts 1:8)

According to Jesus' own words, world evangelism has to be accomplished in the time between His first and second coming. Therefore, there must be an extended period of time involved, a much greater period than that anticipated by the early church which looked for the Lord's return in their lifetime. Since the sad history of the church includes periods of great unfaithfulness to the original message of the Gospel, this period of time has been extended to our own day.

The significance of our own day is that despite the continuing unfaithfulness of much of the visible church, the message of the Gospel is going out into all the Earth. The effect of world evangelism is the only division which has eternal significance—not the division of Jew and Gentile, black and white, male and female, rich and poor—but the division of lost and saved:

> [T]he kingdom of heaven is like unto a net, that was cast into the sea, and gathered of every kind: which, when it was full, they drew to shore, and sat down, and gathered the good into vessels, but cast the bad away. So shall it be at the end of the world: the angels shall come forth, and sever the wicked from among the just, and shall cast them into the furnace of fire: there shall be wailing and gnashing of teeth. (Matthew 13:47-50)

Those who are saved receive new spiritual life which begins now and goes on into eternity. This new life is required to bring in the age of peace and justice promised in the Messianic age. This is why there has to be judgment first. You cannot have a new kind of society without new people. The dismal failure of Communism to produce the better society it promised is a clear witness to this.

JESUS DID NOT FAIL—NOR IS HE GOING TO FAIL!

Therefore, the Christian doctrine of the second coming does not imply that Jesus failed the first time and is coming back down to have another go. Anything but. Jesus succeeded completely when He came the first time, opening up a fountain for cleansing from sin for Jew and Gentile alike through His sacrifice for the sins of the world. He fulfilled the Messianic prophecies to the letter. He was born to a virgin (Isaiah 7:14) in Bethlehem (Micah 5:2). He preached a message of good news to the poor bringing release to those in captivity to sin and sickness (Isaiah 61:1-2). He laid down His life as a sacrifice for the sins of the world, was executed as a transgressor, although without sin Himself, prayed for those responsible for His death, was buried in a rich man's tomb and rose again from the dead on the third day (Psalm 22, Isaiah 53, Zechariah 12:10, Psalm 16:8-11).

All this happened before the destruction of the second temple as prophesied in Daniel 9:25-26. This prophecy in Daniel actually says that "Messiah [shall] be cut off, but not for himself" (speaking of the sacrificial death of Jesus) and that following this "the people of the prince that shall come [i.e., the Romans] shall destroy the city [Jerusalem] and the sanctuary [the Temple]." The fall of Jerusalem would be followed by wars and desolations. As we have seen in the previous chapter, this is a specific prophecy showing that the first coming of the Messiah is followed by the destruction of the Temple and wars and desolations. This counters the argument that because the Messiah was to cause the Jewish people to return to Israel, the

Temple to be rebuilt, and there to be an era of world peace, He cannot be the Messiah since the opposite happened when Jesus came.

Jesus will not fail when He comes again either. At that time, prophecies as yet unfulfilled will be fulfilled. He will come in the clouds of heaven (Daniel 7:13, Mark 14:62) and every eye will see Him (Zechariah 12:10, Revelation 1:7). He will come with the "holy ones" or saints (Zechariah 14:5, Revelation 19:14). The point of His return to Earth will be the Mount of Olives, just outside Jerusalem (Zechariah 14:4, Acts 1:11). He will bring an end to the world conflict that will be raging over Jerusalem and will threaten the world with the final holocaust (Zechariah 12-14, Revelation 16-19). He will destroy the "Babylon" world system responsible for all corruption and wickedness on Earth (Jeremiah 51, Revelation 18). He will set up godly rule from Jerusalem, bringing peace and justice to the nations of the world (Isaiah 2:1-4, Revelation 20:4-6). Following the Millennium (1000 years rule of Messiah), the world will end with one final satanic rebellion against the Lord after which God will create the new heavens and new Earth that will last for eternity (Isaiah 66:22-24, Revelation 20:7-21). For these verses written out, see Appendix.

And the Lord commanded me at that time

to teach you statutes and judgments, that ye

might do them in the land whither ye go over

to possess it.—**Moses** (Deuteronomy 4:14)

CHAPTER 11

IS TORAH THE BRIDGE TO GOD?

———◆———

"OK. So Jesus can be the Savior for the Christians if you like, but we Jews have our own way to God. You go to the middle man; we go straight to the boss!" This is a common response to the kind of argument presented so far in this book. As far as Judaism is concerned, there is no need for a mediator because God reveals Himself directly to Israel through the Torah.[1] Rabbi Emanuel Feldman explains:

> Torah is the mysterious bridge which connects the Jew and God, across which they interact and communicate, and by means of which God fulfills His covenant with His people to sustain them and protect them.[2]

In one article by Rabbi Shraga Simmons, he describes this "mysterious bridge" and how it affects the Jewish people. He states:

> • At Mount Sinai when the Torah was given, the entire Jewish nation—3 million men, women and children "directly experienced divine revelation."

• In addition to the written Torah, God gave the Oral Torah, which in fact preceded the written Torah.

• Torah is the way to self-perfection, and the all night learning of Torah on the festival of Shavuoth is called Tikkun Leil Shavuot, which means "an act of self-perfection on the night of Shavuot."[3]

DIRECT REVELATION OR DIVINE MEDIATION?

Did the entire Jewish nation "directly experience divine revelation"? Rabbi Simmons bases this claim on this verse from Deuteronomy:

> And the LORD spake unto you out of the midst of the fire: ye heard the voice of the words, but saw no similitude; only ye heard a voice. And he declared unto you his covenant, which he commanded you to perform, even ten commandments; and he wrote them upon two tables of stone. (Deuteronomy 4:12-13)

However, the following verse shows that Moses was the mediator through whom God gave the Torah to Israel:

> And the LORD commanded me at that time to teach you statutes and judgments, that ye might do them in the land whither ye go over to possess it. (Deuteronomy 4:14)

This section of Deuteronomy retells the events that took place forty years earlier at Sinai for the benefit of the generation that survived the forty years of wandering in the wilderness and were about to enter the Promised Land.

In the Exodus account of the Torah being given to the generation that came out of Egypt, the emphasis is on the separation of the people from Mount Sinai and from the encounter Moses had with the Lord:

> And Moses brought forth the people out of the camp to meet with God; and they stood at the nether part of the mount. . . .

And the LORD came down upon mount Sinai, on the top of the mount: and the LORD called Moses up to the top of the mount; and Moses went up. And the LORD said unto Moses, Go down, charge the people, lest they break through unto the LORD to gaze, and many of them perish. And let the priests also, which come near to the LORD, sanctify themselves, lest the LORD break forth upon them. (Exodus 19:17, 20-22)

And all the people saw the thunderings, and the lightnings, and the noise of the trumpet, and the mountain smoking: and when the people saw it, they removed, and stood afar off. And they said unto Moses, Speak thou with us, and we will hear: but let not God speak with us, lest we die. (Exodus 20:18-19)

These passages show that the communication of God's commandments did not come directly to three million people of Israel but through the chosen mediator, Moses. In fact, far from being able to come *straight to the boss*, God denied access into His presence to all but a handful of chosen and sanctified men. Moses, in particular, acted as the mediator through whom God spoke to the rest of the people.

WHAT ABOUT THE ORAL TORAH?

Rabbi Simmons writes:

The Oral Torah is not an interpretation of the Written Torah. In fact, the Oral Torah preceded the Written Torah. When the Jewish people stood at Mount Sinai 3,300 years ago, God communicated the 613 commandments, along with a detailed, practical explanation of how to fulfil them. At that point in time, the teachings were entirely oral. It wasn't until 40 years later, just prior to Moses' death and the Jewish people entering the Land of Israel, that Moses wrote the scroll of the written Torah (known as the Five Books of Moses) and gave it to the Jewish people.[4]

Rabbi Simmons says that God gave Moses the Oral Torah at Sinai. This preceded the written Torah and explained how to keep the law. This was not written down but was transmitted by God to Moses orally, then by Moses to Joshua and then passed on by word of mouth from one generation to another from teacher to student in an unbroken chain that is said to lead back to Moses. The Talmud states:

> Moses received the law [Oral Law] on Sinai and delivered it to Joshua; Joshua to the elders [the judges], the elders to the prophets, and the prophets to the Great Synagogue [the scribes in the time of Ezra]. (Tractate Avot 10:1)

The process of writing this down began around 200 AD with the work of Rabbi Judah Hanasi. With the loss of a central authority following the dispersion of the Jewish people, he feared these teachings would be lost, so he went from rabbi to rabbi, writing down what they remembered of the oral traditions. He put those recollections together, edited them, and the result was the Mishna (which means repetition). A commentary on the Mishna called the Gemara was added, the entire compilation being known as the Jerusalem Talmud which was completed around the year 350. Around 500, further writings were compiled in the Babylonian Talmud.

Rabbi Aryeh Kaplan wrote on this subject:

> In many respects, the Oral Torah is *more important than the Written Torah*. It is a foundation of our faith to believe that God gave Moses an oral explanation of the Torah along with the written text.[5] (emphasis added)

The Talmud claims the Oral Torah has equal authority to the Written Law, or even greater authority as seen by this quote:

> The Holy One, Blessed be He, did not make His covenant with Israel except by virtue of the Oral Law.[6] (Gittin 60B)

If this is the case, we would expect to find reference to this fact in the Written Torah. So does the Bible give evidence of the existence of an Oral Torah that was in existence from the time of Moses and was used to interpret the Written Torah throughout the history of Israel recorded in the Bible?

If we examine the text, we find a number of passages in the Bible referring to the words that were *written and read* to Israel but none are to be found about unwritten/oral passages. Consider the following:

> And Moses *wrote all the words of the LORD.* . . . And he took the book of the covenant, and read in the audience of the people: and they said, All that the LORD hath said will we do, and be obedient. (Exodus 24:4, 7; emphasis added; see also Exodus 34:27)

At the end of the book of Deuteronomy, we read about Moses writing the words of the law and putting it in the Ark of the Covenant, but we find nothing about an Oral Torah:

> And it came to pass, when *Moses had made an end of writing the words of this law in a book*, until they were finished, that Moses commanded the Levites, which bare the ark of the covenant of the LORD, saying, Take this book of the law, and put it in the side of the ark of the covenant of the LORD your God, that it may be there for a witness against thee. (Deuteronomy 31:24-26; emphasis added)

The Book of Joshua goes on to tell us that Joshua (to whom Moses is supposed to have communicated the unwritten Oral Torah) possessed a written word, which he read to the people of Israel as they entered the Land. This written word contained all that Moses had passed down:

> And afterward he read *all the words of the law*, the blessings and cursings, *according to all that is written* in the book of the law. *There was not a word of all that Moses commanded, which*

Joshua read not before all the congregation of Israel, with the women, and the little ones, and the strangers that were conversant among them. (Joshua 8:34-35; emphasis added)

If Joshua read all the words of the law and did not leave out a word of all that Moses commanded, where does that leave the Oral Torah? None of these verses in the books of the Torah or in the book of Joshua speak of an unwritten Oral Torah that precedes the written Torah given by God at Mount Sinai. Over and over, we read in the Tenach about *what is written* in the Law of Moses. The Written Law was the basis of God's covenant with Israel. Obedience to the commands written in the law brought God's blessing on Israel; disobedience brought His judgment. The following verses in the Tenach bear witness to this: Exodus 24:4-12, Leviticus 26:46, Numbers 36:13, Deuteronomy 17:18-20, 27:2-26, 28:52-62, 29:20-29, 30:8-10, 31:9-13, 24-26, Joshua 1:7-8, 8:31-35, 23:6, 1 Kings 2:1-4, 2 Kings 22:13-16, 23:2-3, 21-25, 1 Chronicles 16:39-40, 2 Chronicles 23:18, 30:5-16, 31:3, 35:12, Ezra 7:1-10, Nehemiah 8:1-18, 10:28-29, and Daniel 9:3-13. In not one of these passages and nowhere else in the Bible is there any mention of an Oral Torah.

Dr. Daniel Grubner has written:

If there was an Oral Law which God gave to Moses, Moses never mentioned it, nor did Joshua, Ezra, or any other person in the Bible. If it existed, it was not part of God's covenant with Israel. Nor was it relevant to the blessing or judgment of God.

No prophet, priest, or king either mentions it or demonstrates any concern to know it or obey it. It was not relevant to the governance or required worship of Israel. Nor did it play any part in the Instruction of the people or their children.

In other words, on the basis of what is recorded in Tanakh, there was no Oral Law given by God to Moses at Sinai.[7]

So where did the Oral Torah come from? In the period following the return of the Jews from Babylon, it was understood that the reason for the captivity in Babylon was that the people had not kept the laws of the Torah. In order to prevent this from happening again it was decided to *put a fence around the Torah* by putting additional laws in place to prevent the people from inadvertently breaking the Torah. The adding of these laws is justified by the Talmudic command to "make a fence round the Torah" (Aboth 1:1).

Why does the Torah need a fence around it? Rabbi Dr. Epstein explains:

> The Torah is conceived as a garden and its precepts as precious plants. Such a garden is fenced round for the purpose of obviating willful or even unintended damage. Likewise, the precepts of the Torah were to be "fenced" round with additional inhibitions that should have the effect of preserving the original commandments from trespass.[8]

This explanation is affirmed in different places in the Talmud (e.g., "The Rabbis erected a safeguard for a Scriptural law."[9])

In other words, laws were to be added to the original laws in order to make sure that the people of Israel did not break the laws inadvertently. So the Talmud adds a great number of commandments to the commands of the Torah. On this subject of the Sabbath, Rabbi Gil Student writes:

> What does the Torah mean when it (Exodus 20:10) forbids "work" on the sabbath? What work is forbidden and what is not? Without an oral explanation of the details of this forbidden work, it is impossible to know what the Torah means.[10]

On the basis of explaining what "work" is in relation to the Sabbath, the Talmud has divided work up into 39 classes of work:

Sowing, ploughing, reaping, binding sheaves, threshing, winnowing, cleansing crops, grinding, sifting, kneading, baking, shearing wool, washing or beating or dyeing it, spinning, weaving, making two loops, weaving two threads, separating two threads, tying [a knot], loosening [a knot], sewing two stitches, tearing in order to sew two stitches, hunting a gazelle, slaughtering or flaying or salting it or curing its skin, scraping it or cutting it up, writing two letters, erasing in order to write two letters, building, pulling down, putting out a fire, lighting a fire, striking with a hammer and taking out aught from one domain to another.[11]

There are up to 1500 laws on the Sabbath alone comprising over 300 pages of difficult and complex reasoning in the Talmud. Since the average person has neither the time nor the ability to read all of this material, he must rely on the Rabbis to rule on what he may and may not do on the Sabbath. Using these rules to apply to modern life, it is forbidden to switch on a light or any electrical appliance, use public transport, drive a car, press a button on pedestrian crossing, push an invalid chair or a baby buggy outside the home on the Sabbath. There are even instructions on what kind of brush you can use to brush your hair in order to prevent inadvertently pulling out a hair, whether you can eat food in a fridge if you open it and the internal light comes on, and a multitude of other possibilities which are derived from interpreting the teachings of the Talmud.

Josephus, the most important Jewish historian of the first century, described the customs and beliefs of the Pharisees and gives us a clue to the origin of these teachings:

The Pharisees had passed on to the people certain regulations *handed down by former generations and not recorded in the Law of Moses.* And for that reason it is that the Sadducees reject them, and say that we are to esteem those observances to be obligatory which are in the written word, but are not to observe what are derived from the tradition of our forefathers.[12] (emphasis added)

Interestingly, a similar expression "tradition of the elders" is used in the New Testament to describe the oral traditions of the Pharisees, which Jesus rejected as having any authority from God (Mark 7:3 and 5, Matthew 15:2).

Jewish professor Albert Baumgarten wrote:

> The claim that the traditions of the Pharisees were of great antiquity was disputed in the first century by Sadducees, members of the Qumran community and Christians. The Pharisees probably invented the idea that their traditions were ancient to encourage contemporary Jews to join their party.[13]

So how did the Oral Torah arise? In the third and second century BC, the scribes and Pharisees began to develop traditions of how to interpret and apply the Torah, which added laws to the written law. These were passed on to succeeding generations and became known as "the traditions of the fathers/elders." Over time, as the Pharisees claimed to be the true representatives of Judaism, they began to claim that these traditions went all the way back to Moses, rather than the second or third century BC. This led to the idea of a divinely inspired Oral Torah being given to Moses on Sinai, which really has no justification in Scripture or in history.

Following the destruction of the Temple, the Sadducees ceased to have any purpose, being the priestly class, and the Pharisees emerged as the preservers of Judaism. They replaced Temple worship with their own teachings that are the basis of modern Judaism. These teachings were then written down in the Talmud and given divine authority by later rabbis.

So the Talmud becomes equally important or even more important than the Word of God in the Bible. If the Talmud is the summing up of the Oral Torah which was given by God to Moses (and therefore equal to the Word of God) that is fine. But if not, then we have a problem. It means that human tradition and teaching become more important than the Word of God and actually obscures its meaning.

An Orthodox Jew once said to me, "Our religion is ninety percent Talmud and ten percent Tenach."

I repeated that to another Orthodox Jew who said, "He is wrong there. Ninety percent is much too low for the Talmud!" Placing emphasis on the Talmud means that Jewish people are less inclined to read the Bible for themselves and to seek God for its meaning. On one occasion when I was working as a teacher at the Hasmonean School, I was sitting in a classroom during the lunch hour on my own reading from Isaiah in my Bible. An Orthodox boy came in and saw what I was doing and was quite shocked. "We would never sit down and read the Bible like that," he said. "You have to read it with the commentaries, otherwise you cannot understand it."

WHERE DOES THE NEW COVENANT FIT IN?

In the time of the New Testament, there was no Oral Law written down. However, "the traditions of the fathers" taught by the Pharisees were very much in evidence. Jesus told His disciples to "beware of the leaven (teaching) of the Pharisees" (Matthew 16:6). He said of the scribes and Pharisees of His day, "they bind heavy burdens and grievous to be borne, and lay them on men's shoulders" (Matthew 23:4).

In Mark 7:6-9, Jesus quoted Isaiah 29:13 to illustrate the point:

> This people honoureth me with their lips, but their heart is far from me. Howbeit in vain do they worship me, teaching for doctrines the commandments of men. For laying aside the commandment of God, ye hold the tradition of men, as the washing of pots and cups: and many other such like things ye do. And he said unto them, Full well ye reject the commandment of God, that ye may keep your own tradition.

He is saying that the added laws which were brought in to "make a fence around the Torah" were not given to Moses by God at Sinai, and are no more than "the commandments of men" and should not be treated as "commandments of God."

It is interesting that the Karaite Jews, who uphold the written Torah but deny the validity of the Oral Torah, use the same verse from Isaiah 29 to give their reason for rejecting the Talmud. Significantly, the verses which precede Isaiah 29:13 prophesy a time coming when spiritual blindness would come upon Israel causing the words of the book to become sealed:

> Stay yourselves [pause], and wonder; cry ye out, and cry: they are drunken, but not with wine; they stagger, but not with strong drink. For the LORD hath poured out upon you the spirit of deep sleep, and hath closed your eyes: the prophets and your rulers, the seers hath he covered. And the vision of all is become unto you as the words of a book that is sealed, which men deliver to one that is learned, saying, Read this, I pray thee: and he saith, I cannot; for it is sealed. (Isaiah 29:9-11)

In other words, something will happen which will cause a spiritual blindness and slumber to come upon Israel that will make the words of the book (the Bible and particularly its prophetic word) like a sealed book that cannot be understood. Is this brought about by the added laws and the Talmudic interpretations which give authority to the rabbis to be the sole interpreters of the Scriptures?

Paul wrote to the Corinthians:

> [B]ut their minds were blinded: for until this day remaineth the same vail untaken away in the reading of the old testament; which vail is done away in Christ. But even unto this day, when Moses is read, the vail is upon their heart. (2 Corinthians 3:14-15)

What Paul is saying here is that the words of the Hebrew Bible point to Yeshua, Jesus, as the Promised Messiah. However, the majority ruling of the rabbis is that Jesus is not the Messiah and that Jews should not even consider any opinion which points in this direction. As long as Jewish people submit to this ruling, then the "veil" will remain on their hearts, and they will not be able to see Jesus in the

Scriptures. When they turn to the Lord in repentance and faith in Jesus as the Messiah, then this veil will be removed. From the point of view of the believer in Jesus, the writings of the Talmud form a veil that blinds Jewish people to the truth of the Gospel.

According to rabbinic Judaism, the Oral Law is necessary in order to understand the Written Law. Therefore, the Torah on its own is insufficient to guide us. Actually, there is a truth that the Torah needs another book to be added to it. On its own, there are issues in the Torah which cannot be resolved.

Since the fall of the Second Temple and the dispersion of the Jewish people, many of the commandments in the written Torah have become impossible for people to keep. All of the commandments concerning the tabernacle, the priesthood, and the sacrifices cannot be kept by anyone today. This involves a large amount of the text of the Torah—most of Exodus 26-40 and Leviticus 1-10. The instructions concerning the keeping of the feasts (Leviticus 16-17, 23) are only kept in part by Orthodox Jews because of the absence of the tabernacle/Temple, priesthood, and sacrifices today.

Rabbis today acknowledge this. In his book *The Handbook of Jewish Thought*, Rabbi Kaplan states:

> There is a tradition that God included 613 commandments in the Torah. Of these, 248 are positive, while 365 are negative. Many of these commandments, however, deal with the laws of purity and sacrifice, and were thus only applicable when the Holy Temple stood in Jerusalem. Therefore, of all the commandments, only 369 apply today. Of these, 126 are positive, and 243 are negative. Even of these, however, many only pertain to special cases or circumstances. The total number of commandments which apply to everyone under all conditions is 270. Of these, 48 are positive, and 222 are negative.[14]

So from the 613 commandments in the Torah, Rabbi Kaplan acknowledges that only 270 are to be for today.

After the destruction of the Temple in 70 AD, Rabbi Yohanan ben Zakkai established the academy at Yavneh where he set up a way to preserve Judaism without sacrifices, priesthood and Temple, saying in effect that good deeds replaced the sacrifices of the Torah as the means of gaining atonement for sin. Jewish critics of Christianity accuse Christians (Paul in particular) of changing the Torah. But so did Yohanan ben Zakkai. In fact, Judaism resolved the problem caused by the destruction of the Temple by changing the Torah. In effect, a new religion emerged as a Jewish commentary on the work of ben Zakkai admits:

> Judaism did not disappear (with the destruction of the Temple). What it did is transform itself. From a religion centered around Temple, priesthood and sacrifice it became a religion centered around Torah study, prayer at home and in the synagogue, and *gemilut hasadim* [acts of loving kindness]. From a historical point of view it is accurate to say that *Biblical and Rabbinic Judaism are two different, though of course related, religions.* It was Rabban Yohanan ben Zakkai more than anyone else who made this possible.[15] (emphasis added)

Today, Orthodox Jews zealously keep aspects of the Torah which are possible to keep—kosher food regulations, Sabbath observance, ritual purity, festivals, and holy days. They add numerous laws on these subjects that are found in the Talmud. But this does not answer the question as to why God has permitted more than 1900 years to pass, during which time it has been impossible to keep so many aspects of the Torah.

Because so much of the written code of the Torah is impossible to keep literally today, traditional Jews need the Talmud and the Law Codes and traditions interpreted by the rabbis in order to know how to apply these laws today. The alternative view is to say that we need the Holy Spirit given through the Messiah to show us how to keep God's commands and walk in His ways. It is not a coincidence that forty years before the Temple was destroyed and the way to keep so many of the Torah commands was permanently lost, Jesus the Messiah offered His own blood to usher in the New Covenant and replace the need for the Levitical priesthood and the sacrifices. He also prophesied that the Jewish people would be scattered to the nations, following the fall of the Temple. So much of the Torah requires Israel to be living in the Land with the Temple/Tabernacle standing, in a basically agricultural society. Once the Temple was destroyed and the people scattered from the land, much of the Torah became impossible to keep. By contrast Jesus' teaching gives us universal commandments which can be kept by all people living anywhere in the world.

Lecturer and evangelist to the Jewish people Arnold Fruchtenbaum has written:

> The clear-cut teaching of the New Testament is that the Law of Moses has been rendered inoperative with the death of the Messiah. In other words, the Law, in its totality, no longer has authority over any individual. First of all, this is evident, from Romans 10:4: "For Christ is the end of the law for righteousness to every one that believeth." Very clearly, Christ is the end of the Law, and that includes all 613 commandments; hence the Law has ceased to function. There is no justification through it.

> In Galatians 2:16 we read: "knowing that a man is not justified by the works of the law, but by the faith of Jesus Christ, even we have believed in Jesus Christ, that we might be justified by the faith of Christ, and not by the works of the law: for by the works of the law shall no flesh be justified." . . .

> Thus, it should be very evident that the Law has come to an end in the Messiah and cannot function in justification or sanctification. For the believer especially it has been rendered inoperative. The remaining verses, however, show that the Law has ceased to function for all. . . .

The Law of Moses has been disannulled, and we are now under a new law. This new law is called: *the law of Christ* in Galatians 6:2 and *the law of the Spirit of life* in Romans 8:2. This is a brand new law, totally separate from the Law of Moses.[16]

As we have already seen in chapter nine of this book, Jeremiah prophesied the coming of the New Covenant that will be different from and replace the covenant with Moses:

> Behold, the days come, saith the LORD, that I will make a new covenant with the house of Israel, and with the house of Judah: not according to the covenant that I made with their fathers in the day that I took them by the hand to bring them out of the land of Egypt; which my covenant they brake, although I was an husband unto them, saith the LORD: but this shall be the covenant that I will make with the house of Israel; After those days, saith the LORD, I will put my law in their inward parts, and write it in their hearts; and will be their God, and they shall be my people. And they shall teach no more every man his neighbour, and every man his brother, saying, Know the LORD: for they shall all know me, from the least of them unto the greatest of them, saith the LORD: for I will forgive their iniquity, and I will remember their sin no more. (Jeremiah 31:31-34)

Quoting this passage in Hebrews 8, the writer concludes:

> In that he saith, A new covenant, he hath made the first old. Now that which decayeth and waxeth old is ready to vanish away. (Hebrews 8:13)

The New Covenant, which corresponds to the law of Christ that Arnold Fruchtenbaum writes about, has many similarities to the Law of Moses because both are given by the same God. In the Sermon on the Mount (Matthew 5-7), Jesus said, "Think not that I am come to destroy the law, or the prophets: I am not come to destroy, but to fulfil" (Matthew 5:17).

He took the commandments from the Torah and spoke about the need to deal with the inward attitudes which cause evil behavior. Not only should we not commit murder, but we should not be angry without a cause, we should seek reconciliation as soon as possible with anyone we are out of fellowship with. Not only should we not commit adultery, we should not look at a woman lustfully. We should love our enemies and pray for those who hate us (Matthew 5:21-48). He told His disciples:

> Ye are the light of the world. A city that is set on an hill cannot be hid. . . . Let your light so shine before men, that they may see your good works, and glorify your Father which is in heaven. (Matthew 5:14, 16)

We find that the ten commandments are restated in the New Testament:

> Owe no man any thing, but to love one another: for he that loveth another hath fulfilled the law. For this, Thou shalt not commit adultery, Thou shalt not kill, Thou shalt not steal, Thou shalt not bear false witness, Thou shalt not covet; and if there be any other commandment, it is briefly comprehended in this saying, namely, Thou shalt love thy neighbour as thyself. Love worketh no ill to his neighbour: therefore love is the fulfilling of the law. (Romans 13:8-10)

If we look at the New Testament, we find that worship of God only is called for fifty times; idolatry is forbidden twelve times; profanity four times; honour of father and mother is commanded six times; adultery is forbidden twelve; theft six; false witness four; and covetousness, nine times.

The New Testament book of Hebrews shows how the ceremonial side of the Torah (priesthood, tabernacle, sacrifices) is fulfilled in Jesus Christ, the Messiah (see Hebrews 7-10). He is the High Priest who has made the final sacrifice for sin through shedding His blood, which has been accepted by God. As the writer to the Hebrews states:

> And almost all things are by the law purged with blood; and without shedding of blood is no remission. (Hebrews 9:22)

The items in the tabernacle and even the High Priest's vestments all point to Jesus (see Hebrews 7-10). In fact, in this interpretation, biblical Christianity can claim more continuity with Torah teaching than modern Judaism that replaces the sacrifices with prayer and good works in order to atone for sin.

The sacrifice of the Lord Jesus for the sins of the world deals with the fundamental problem, which is actually made clear by the Torah. God is holy and separate from human beings because the human race is sinful. Therefore, God cannot dwell with them. Under the Torah, we read how God provided a temporary solution to this problem. In Leviticus 16, we read about how He provided atonement for the sins of the people of Israel on Yom Kippur, the Day of Atonement. If we follow through this passage, we see clearly that God requires a mediator in order to relate to His people. In this case, it is the High Priest who first has to make sacrifices for his own sins before he could enter into the Holy of Holies to offer the required sacrifice to cover the sins of the people.

This whole process has now been replaced by the sacrifice of the Lord Jesus as the book of Hebrews makes clear:

> But Christ being come an high priest of good things to come, by a greater and more perfect tabernacle, not made with hands, that is to say, not of this building; neither by the blood of goats and calves, but by his own blood he entered in once into the holy place, having obtained eternal redemption for us. For if the blood of bulls and of goats, and the ashes of an heifer sprinkling the unclean, sanctifieth to the purifying of the flesh: how much more shall the blood of Christ, who through the eternal Spirit offered himself without spot to God, purge your conscience from dead works to serve the

living God? And for this cause he is the mediator of the new testament, that by means of death, for the redemption of the transgressions that were under the first testament, they which are called might receive the promise of eternal inheritance. (Hebrews 9:11-15)

By this means, the New Covenant sealed with the blood of the Messiah has now replaced the former covenant given to Moses.

We also find in the Torah a number of civil laws applying to crime and punishment, agriculture, warfare, and so on. Putting these civil laws into action requires Israel to be a self-governing people living in the land of Israel. During the time of the Diaspora when Jewish people lived as a minority people in other people's lands, they were not in a position to make laws that would be binding on the lands in which they lived. They could keep those aspects of the Torah that were possible to keep within their communities. These include circumcision, Sabbath observance, and kosher food laws, which have actually become central to modern Judaism and the things that define the Jewish community.

If we are not able to keep the commandments of God, we are left in a state of condemnation. The Bible shows us that our failure to keep God's commandments causes the gulf that separates us from God. The Bible also shows our need of a mediator to bridge this gulf. This is why God promised He would make a New Covenant with the house of Israel, not because He found fault with the old one but because of the impossibility of keeping it. In his letter to believers in Messiah, living in Galatia, Paul described the Torah as "our schoolmaster [tutor] to bring us unto Christ, that we might be justified by faith" (Galatians 3:24). By this, He meant that the Torah shows us we cannot achieve "self-perfection" and that a huge gulf exists between what God requires and what we achieve. It was for this very reason that I turned to the Messiah on January 1st 1970 when I realized I had broken God's commandments and was under His judgment.

The Torah shows us that we all fall short of the glory of God and need to be made right with God by repentance and faith in the sacrifice God has appointed. Under the Old Covenant, this was through the blood of the animals offered on Yom Kippur. Under the New Covenant, it is through the blood of the Messiah. In this way, Messiah Jesus becomes our bridge to God, fulfilling His Word,

> I am the way, the truth, and the life: no man cometh unto the Father, but by me. (John 14:6)

When speaking to Nicodemus, a learned rabbi of His day, Jesus said that in order to enter into this New Covenant—"Ye must be born again" (John 3:7), not physically but spiritually—an experience also prophesied in Ezekiel:

> A new heart also will I give you, and a new spirit will I put within you: and I will take away the stony heart out of your flesh, and I will give you an heart of flesh. And I will put my spirit within you, and cause you to walk in my statutes, and ye shall keep my judgments, and do them. (Ezekiel 36:26-27)

Just as the covenant at Sinai had to be mediated through God's chosen servant, Moses, so the New Covenant had to be mediated through a Prophet like Moses (see Deuteronomy 18:15-18). Isaiah reveals this one would be more than a prophet. Although He would be born as a child, "his name shall be called Wonderful, Counsellor, The mighty God, The everlasting Father, The Prince of Peace" (Isaiah 9:6).

As we have seen in chapter six of this book, Isaiah went on to describe how this anointed Servant of the Lord would be put to death for the sins of the people:

> All we like sheep have gone astray; we have turned every one to his own way; and the LORD hath laid on him the iniquity of us all. . . . he was cut off out of the land of the living: for the transgression of my people was he stricken. (Isaiah 53:6, 8)

Yeshua, Jesus, is the Messiah of whom Moses and the Prophets spoke, who has mediated the New Covenant through which we can find the true bridge to God. Through His death and resurrection, He has paid the price required for sin and made it possible for all humanity, Jewish and Gentile, to come to know God's forgiveness and eternal life. Those who truly accept Him as Messiah, Savior and Lord experience the new birth which Jesus spoke about to Nicodemus that enables us by the Holy Spirit to walk in newness of life and gives us the desire to keep His commandments. Although we remain liable to sin and still fall short of the glory of God, the blood Jesus Christ shed is sufficient to cover our sins and to give us peace with God so that we know when we appear before God on the Day of Judgment, He will receive us into eternal life in His kingdom which shall never pass away.

CHAPTER 12

THE MESSIAH AND THE END OF DAYS

———◆———

Rabbi Pinchas Winston wrote:

> We are living in very turbulent times, to say the least.
> . . . Now, more than ever before over the last 50 years,
> the Jewish people, and even the world in general, need a
> savior. We need someone who can, somehow—perhaps even
> mystically—bring about more than just a tenuous ceasefire
> between two warring peoples. We need someone who can,
> once and for all, bring an end to all human conflict, especially
> in the Middle East.
>
> And, if he can do that—a tall order—then perhaps he would
> also be able to destroy whatever other evil exists in the world.
> As he engineers this long-dreamed-of world peace, let him
> make unethical and immoral behavior a thing of the past,
> too. In other words, this savior, if he is truly a savior, should
> usher in a permanent utopian society where virtuous living
> is the main theme and second- (if not first) nature.
>
> And, what shall we call this modern-day hero of Biblical
> proportions?

In Judaism, he has always been called "Moshiach" (Messiah), "the anointed one," because, as a Jewish king he is to be anointed upon taking office, so-to-speak.[1]

As we have seen in this book, the major task of the Messiah according to rabbinic Judaism is to bring peace to Israel and the world. Rabbi Winston acknowledges that bringing peace and an end to human conflict, particularly in the Middle East is "a tall order." Some might say it is an impossibility, given the level of hostility that exists in the Middle East.

The Bible does say that there will be peace and justice in Israel in the last days (Isaiah 2:1-4). The question is how will Israel and the world reach this state?

Events in Israel over the last hundred years are a remarkable fulfillment of Biblical prophecy. Jewish people have returned to Israel from countries around the world, coming from the north, south, east and west as the prophets had said they would:

> And he shall set up an ensign for the nations, and shall assemble the outcasts of Israel, and gather together the dispersed of Judah from the four corners of the earth. (Isaiah 11:12)

> Fear not: for I am with thee: I will bring thy seed from the east, and gather thee from the west; I will say to the north, Give up; and to the south, Keep not back: bring my sons from far, and my daughters from the ends of the earth. (Isaiah 43:5-6)

> Hear the word of the LORD, O ye nations, and declare it in the isles afar off, and say, He that scattered Israel will gather him, and keep him, as a shepherd doth his flock. (Jeremiah 31:10)

Ezekiel prophesied a time when the land, which had become desolate, would become fertile again as the people of Israel return to it:

But ye, O mountains of Israel, ye shall shoot forth your branches, and yield your fruit to my people of Israel; for they are at hand to come. (Ezekiel 36:8)

During the time when the Jewish people were out of the land, the rainfall decreased to the point where the land did become barren and unfruitful as it was described by travelers in the 19th century. Mark Twain described the land in 1867 in his book *The Innocents Abroad*:

Of all the lands there are for dismal scenery, I think Palestine must be the prince . . . It is a hopeless, dreary, heart broken land . . . Palestine sits in sackcloth and ashes. Over it broods the spell of a curse that has withered its fields and fettered its energies. . . . Palestine is desolate and unlovely.[2]

As Jewish people began to return to the land, the rains began to return with the heaviest rains recorded in 1948, the year of Israel's rebirth as a nation. Millions of trees were planted on the hills, and the desert places began to be irrigated and farmed.

The prophecy of Ezekiel speaks of the physical return of the Jewish people to the land and the spiritual rebirth which they will experience at the time of the end:

For I will take you from among the heathen, and gather you out of all countries, and will bring you into your own land. Then will I sprinkle clean water upon you, and ye shall be clean: from all your filthiness, and from all your idols, will I cleanse you. A new heart also will I give you, and a new spirit will I put within you: and I will take away the stony heart out of your flesh, and I will give you an heart of flesh. And I will put my spirit within you, and cause you to walk in my statutes, and ye shall keep my judgments, and do them. And ye shall dwell in the land that I gave to your fathers; and ye shall be my people, and I will be your God. (Ezekiel 36:24-28)

The physical rebirth of Israel has happened in our time. The Bible indicates there will also be a spiritual rebirth as Israel looks to the Messiah.

The physical rebirth of Israel as a Jewish homeland is one of the most extraordinary events of modern times. Israel's first Prime Minister, David Ben Gurion, famously said, "In Israel, in order to be a realist you must believe in miracles." Israel's establishment and survival against all the odds is a sign of something miraculous taking place. This started with Israel's victory over seven Arab armies that attacked the Jewish state at birth in 1948 and has continued with many signs of divine intervention in wars which have taken place since 1967, 1973, and up to the present time.

The Bible also speaks of a time of trouble in the last days before the return of the Messiah. On October 12th, 2015, Israeli President Rivlin addressed the Knesset with apocalyptic terms:

> Lately we have witnessed more and more attempts by political leaders, and others, to turn the Israeli-Palestinian conflict into a religious conflict. From such a conflict, there would be no return. A war of Armageddon, Jihad, or the end of days. The attempts to stoke the fire of conflict, by passionate fundamentalists is an attempt to set fire to this earth upon which we all sit.[3]

Looking at these events taking place, some rabbis in Israel have hinted in public that the Messiah is "just around the corner." Rabbi Amar said:

> [W]hen the Messiah needs to come, God will incite nations against each other, until, against their will, there will be a war. . . . "It is also written that before the Messiah comes, Israel will suffer greatly from the sons of Ishmael (Arabs) and they will succeed in antagonising us. We are at a crossroads and we need to pray to God to redeem us. We have to wake up and repent or, if not, God forbid, the Ishmaelites will overcome

us." . . . Therefore . . . we should have great inspiration to wake up and repent.[4]

Israel 365 bookstore[5] advertises a number of books giving a Jewish interpretation of the end times. For example, *Survival Guide for the End of Days* by Rabbi Pinchas Winston is promoted with the words:

> The Hebrew Scripture is full of references to the End Times and the coming of Mashiach (the Jewish Messiah). The Mashiach will unify the Jewish people and gather all the exiles back to the holy land of Israel. He will rebuild the Temple in Jerusalem and revive the dead. The entire world will recognize the one true God, and the purpose of God's creation on earth will be fulfilled. But all of this will only happen after a great war.[6]

Promoting the book *Not Just another Scenario* by Rabbi Winston, the Israel 365 bookstore states:

> The prophet Zachariah spoke about "A day of the Lord" during which Jerusalem would be ravaged, mountains would split and streams would flow uphill. What this prophecy tells us is that the times of the Messiah will be filled with strange natural disasters and events that we can neither anticipate nor understand. Pinchas Winston's book is an attempt to peek behind that curtain of prophecy and show us what a real-life apocalypse might look like in today's world.[7]

Rabbi Winston has connected Russia's move into Syria with the war of Gog and Magog, seeing it as a sign "as so many End-of-Days elements start to come together just north of the Jewish State."[8]

The war of Gog and Magog is prophesied in the book of Ezekiel 38-39. In this war, a great power to the north of Israel assembles an armed coalition to invade Israel from the north. The armies are led by "Gog, the land of Magog, the chief prince of Meshech and Tubal" (Ezekiel 38:2). Bible students have identified this power with Russia, coming from "thy place out of the north parts" (Ezekiel 38:15), in alliance with a number of countries including Persia (Iran) and Togarmah (Turkey). Interestingly, at the time of writing this chapter (January 2017) these three countries are hosting a peace conference to resolve the conflict in Syria. All three have troops engaged in Syria, and Russia has said it will set up a permanent military base in Tartus, Syria. In the prophecy of Ezekiel, this alliance of nations invades Israel "in the latter days" after the Jewish people have been regathered from the nations to the land of Israel. This combined army is supernaturally destroyed by the intervention of God "on the mountains of Israel" causing the Holy Spirit to be poured out on Israel.

Another book called *Working Towards Moshiach* (Messiah) by Roy Neuberger refers to "a difficult time" based on "Zechariah's apocalyptic vision" and "gives the tools needed to face the coming chaos and reach the final redemption."[9]

Zechariah does, in fact, give some amazingly accurate information about the situation around Jerusalem at the end of days. About 2500 years ago, he prophesied that the status of Jerusalem would be a focal point of attention for Israel, the surrounding nations, and even the whole world:

> Behold, I will make Jerusalem a cup of trembling unto all the people round about . . . a burdensome stone for all people. (Zechariah 12:2-3)

Following the establishment of the State of Israel in 1948, Jerusalem was a divided city. The western part was in Israel, and the historic Old City (where the Temple stood) was in the eastern part, ruled by Jordan. Since the Six Day War of 1967, Israel has ruled over Jerusalem as a united city. Zechariah 14 goes on to describe the end time battle for Jerusalem, "For I will gather all nations against Jerusalem to battle."

As far as the Muslims are concerned, *they* should rule Jerusalem. At the present time, there is a proposal agreed by the world powers and the UN to resolve the Arab-Israeli conflict through the "two-state solution" which means setting up a Palestinian state in the territories occupied by Israel in the Six Day War of 1967. This includes Jerusalem, which has been a central issue in discussions over the division of the territory.

Israel's Prime Minister Netanyahu has said that Jerusalem remains the indivisible capital of Israel and should remain a united city ruled by Israel. The Palestinians, backed by the Arab Muslim nations, want a Palestinian state with its capital in the eastern part of Jerusalem. Palestinian Authority leader, Mahmoud Abbas, has declared, "One day, a young Palestinian will raise the Palestinian flag over Jerusalem, the eternal capital of the state of Palestine!"[10]

All of this ties in with the prophecy of Zechariah that Jerusalem will be a "burdensome stone" to all nations (i.e. the status of Jerusalem will be a matter of international concern) in the last days of this age. This will lead to the final conflict which will draw the hostile nations against Israel and Jerusalem. The prophet Joel also speaks of this as he prophesies of the nations seeking to divide up the land of Israel and thereby coming under the judgment of God (Joel 3:1-2).

Zechariah describes how the Lord intervenes on Israel's behalf at a time when the nations gather together against Jerusalem:

> And I will pour upon the house of David, and upon the inhabitants of Jerusalem, the spirit of grace and of supplications: and they shall look upon me whom they have pierced, and they shall mourn for him, as one mourneth for his only son, and shall be in bitterness for him, as one that is in bitterness for his firstborn. (Zechariah 12:10)

Here we have a prophecy of one who has been "pierced" and who comes to save the remnant of Israel both physically and spiritually in the last days of this age. This speaks of Yeshua the Messiah who came once to save us from our sins by His death when He was "pierced" (died by crucifixion). At this time of great crisis, the people will look on Yeshua as Savior and turn to Him for salvation. Then the Lord will come and stand on the Mount of Olives and defeat the armies coming against Israel and set up His Messianic kingdom on Earth (Zechariah 14).

This, of course, is not the rabbinic interpretation of prophecy. In the view of rabbinic Jewish writers, the Messiah will come as a great human leader who will sort out the mess of the world, save Israel from their enemies, and create world peace. He is not a divine person and certainly not the Lord Jesus returning in power to judge the world and bring in His Messianic kingdom. In 1976, Rabbi Aryeh Kaplan wrote a book titled *The Real Messiah* in which he attacked the idea that Jesus is the Messiah and looked for the Messiah to come as a great man bringing peace to the world.

Rabbi Kaplan says the restoration of Israel is a sign of the coming Messiah, "After 2000 years of suffering and prayer, we are once again in control of our ancient homeland."[11] He claims this shows "we are living in an age where almost all the Jewish prophecies regarding the prelude to the Messianic Age are coming to pass."[12] He also acknowledges that the Messianic Age may bring trouble:

> The rapid changes on both a technological and sociological level will result in a great social upheaval. The cataclysmic changes will result in considerable suffering, often referred to as the *Chevley Moshiach* or Birthpangs of the Messiah. If the Messiah comes with miracles these changes may be avoided, but the great changes involved in his coming in a natural manner may make these changes inevitable.[13]

According to Rabbi Kaplan, the coming Messiah will be a "mortal human being born normally of human parents"[14] who will change the course of history. He states further:

> We have seen, for example, how an evil genius like Hitler literally hypnotised an entire nation, bringing it to do things that normally would be unthinkable in a civilized society. If such a power exists for evil, it [another power] must certainly exist for good.[15]

Rabbi Kaplan believes this Messiah will sort out the problems of the present world by his incredible personality that will change the course of history:

> Now, imagine a charismatic leader greater than any other in man's history. Imagine a political genius surpassing all others. With the vast communication networks now at our disposal, he could spread his message to the entire world and change the very fabric of society.[16]

He describes one possible way the Messiah could come to power:

> One possible scenario could involve the Middle East situation. This is a problem that involves all the world powers. Now imagine a Jew, a Tzadik [literally a "righteous one"] solving this thorny problem. It would not be inconceivable that such a demonstration of statesmanship and political genius would place him in a position of world leadership. The major powers would listen to such an individual.[17]

He goes on to describe how he would regather the exiles to Israel, cause the Temple to be rebuilt, and teach all mankind to live in peace and follow God's teachings. He concludes:

> As society reaches toward perfection and the world becomes increasingly G-dly, men will begin to explore the transcendental more and more. As the prophet said (Isaiah 11:9), "For all the earth shall be full of the knowledge of G-d, as the waters cover the sea." More and more people will achieve the mystical union of prophecy, as foretold (Joel 3:1), "And it shall come to pass afterward that I will pour out My spirit on all flesh, and your sons and your daughters shall prophesy."[18]

Is such a hoped for Messiah about to appear on the world stage and by his charismatic personality inspire the world to peace and following God? Or are current events preparing the way for a more sinister figure to appear? Bible prophecies in Daniel and in Revelation and other books of the New Testament point to the coming of one described as the "lawless one," "the man of sin" (2 Thessalonians 2:3), and also known as the Beast or Antichrist. He will make a covenant with Israel (Daniel 9:27, Isaiah 28:14-22), which will offer peace and safety, but then break down and bring in the final time of "Jacob's trouble" (Jeremiah 30:7) or the Great Tribulation (Matthew 24:15-31).

This Messiah that Rabbi Kaplan is heralding may turn out to be the anti-Messiah or Antichrist whom the Bible says will come in the last days of this age. For this reason, the issue of interpreting prophecy is not just an academic one for scholars to debate about, but it is a vital one for everyone to understand in order to avoid being deceived by the world's final false Messiah.

Jewish messianic hopes center on a great man coming to make world peace and rescue Israel, but the biblical prophecies show this is a vain hope and will lead to deep disillusion and betrayal.

In the last days of this age, there will be a worldwide crisis that will focus on the Arab-Israeli conflict and the question of who rules Jerusalem. Already, this is the main area of world concern with more UN resolutions being passed on this issue than any other trouble spot on Earth. For religious, economic, and political reasons, this crisis will remain the focus in the minds of the whole world in the last days, and the search for a peace settlement will be of prime importance. Today, the major nations of the world (the USA, EU, and Russia) backed by the organization which represents all nations (the UN) have been trying in vain to negotiate a peace plan for the Middle East.

Prophecies in the book of Daniel indicate that the coming Antichrist will be the one who makes this peace settlement:

> And after threescore and two weeks shall Messiah be cut off, but not for himself: and the people of the prince that shall come shall destroy the city and the sanctuary; and the end thereof shall be with a flood, and unto the end of the war desolations are determined. And he shall confirm the covenant with many for one week: and in the midst of the week he

shall cause the sacrifice and the oblation to cease, and for the overspreading of abominations he shall make it desolate, even until the consummation, and that determined shall be poured upon the desolate. (Daniel 9:26-27)

This prophecy speaks first of the true Messiah, who will be cut off dying not for Himself but for the sins of the world before the event of the destruction of the Second Temple (see chapter nine). This will be followed by a long period of wars and desolations of Jerusalem until the final seven year period when "he" will make a covenant with many for "one week" (a "week" in this context means a period of seven years). According to the line of interpretation I am taking here, the one who makes this covenant is the "prince to come," who is identified as the antichrist or beast in the New Testament. He is identified with "the people" who were responsible for the destruction of the Temple (the Romans). This gives rise to the view that he will come out of a revived Roman entity in the last days, which many associate with the EU or the UN. This passage indicates this will be a false peace covenant which will break down halfway through the "week" (i.e., after 3 ½ years), leading to the prophesied time of trouble.

Daniel 11 indicates that the covenant being worked out will be based on deceit:

And in his estate shall stand up a vile person, to whom they shall not give the honour of the kingdom: but he shall come in *peaceably,* and obtain the kingdom by *flatteries.* (Daniel 11:21; emphasis added)

And both these kings' hearts shall be to do mischief, and they shall speak lies at one table; but it shall not prosper: for yet the end shall be at the time appointed. (Daniel 11:27)

While these prophecies were partially fulfilled through Antiochus Epiphanes at the time of the Maccabees, there will be a further fulfilment of this prophecy in the last days. Through a mixture of promises of peace and deceit, the Antichrist will succeed in persuading Israel and the Arab nations to make a peace settlement which will actually leave him with the controlling power over Jerusalem.

> Wherefore hear the word of the LORD, ye scornful men, that rule this people which is in Jerusalem. Because ye have said, We have made a covenant with death, and with hell are we at agreement; when the overflowing scourge shall pass through, it shall not come unto us: for we have made lies our refuge, and under falsehood have we hid ourselves: therefore thus saith the Lord God, Behold, I lay in Zion for a foundation a stone, a tried stone, a precious corner stone, a sure foundation: he that believeth shall not make haste. Judgment also will I lay to the line, and righteousness to the plummet: and the hail shall sweep away the refuge of lies, and the waters shall overflow the hiding place. And your covenant with death shall be disannulled, and your agreement with hell shall not stand; when the overflowing scourge shall pass through, then ye shall be trodden down by it. From the time that it goeth forth it shall take you: for morning by morning shall it pass over, by day and by night: and it shall be a vexation only to understand the report. (Isaiah 28:14-19)

This "covenant with death" will be made by Israel to gain protection from "the overflowing scourge," the threat of invasion and annihilation. However, it will not stand because it is based on lies and falsehood. The phrase "the waters shall overflow the hiding place" points to the very thing Israel feared happening, an enemy invasion and occupation. This will lead to the final event of this age, Armageddon, which will cause the "report" (the news) to be terrible.

In both of the prophecy of Daniel 9:27 and Isaiah 28:14-19, there are those who do not enter into this false peace covenant. In Daniel 9, the Antichrist makes the covenant with "some" but not all. In Isaiah 28:16, there are those who do not act rashly but put their trust in God who says: "Behold, I lay in Zion for a foundation a stone, a tried stone, a precious corner stone, a sure foundation." Psalm 118:22-23, a Messianic Psalm, also has a reference to a stone:

> The stone which the builders refused is become the head stone of the corner. This is the LORD's doing; it is marvellous in our eyes.

This verse is used to point to Jesus as Messiah who suffered rejection and exaltation. It occurs in the New Testament more than any other Old Testament Scripture, in three of the Gospels (Matthew 21:42, Mark 12:10, Luke 20:17), in Acts 4:11, and in 1 Peter 2:6-7.

There is a Jewish story relating to this verse that as the builders were putting the great hewn stones of Solomon's Temple in place, they came across a stone that had an odd shape and did not fit anywhere. So they rejected it and put it on the rubbish heap. As they came to the end of their building, they found an odd-shaped space at the head of the corner. One of the builders who had been there at the beginning of the work remembered the odd-shaped stone, and they looked on the rubbish heap and found it. It was a perfect fit for the odd-shaped space they had left at the head of the corner.

This story has an amazing message in relation to the Messianic claim of Jesus. When He came the first time, He did not fit the idea of the Messiah that many Jewish people had, and so He was put on the rubbish heap spiritually and rejected. At the end of days as the final conflict rages around Jerusalem, the Jewish remnant will understand He is the only one who can fit the empty space in their lives and fulfill their hopes of the Messiah. Then He will return and take up His place of honor and deliver Israel from destruction and create world peace.

When the armies of the world gather together against Jerusalem to battle, God says:

> And I will pour upon the house of David, and upon the inhabitants of Jerusalem, the spirit of grace and of supplications: and they shall look upon me whom they have pierced, and they shall mourn for him, as one mourneth for

his only son, and shall be in bitterness for him, as one that is in bitterness for his firstborn. (Zechariah 12:10)

The one who has been pierced speaks of the Messiah Jesus who died by having His hands and feet pierced. As the people look to Him, they mourn for their sins and the years of separation the Jewish people have had from their Messiah who loves them and gave Himself for Israel and the world in order to redeem them. This will lead to repentance and cleansing through the blood of the Messiah as Zechariah 13:1 says:

In that day there shall be a fountain opened to the house of David and to the inhabitants of Jerusalem for sin and for uncleanness.

Following this Zechariah says:

Then shall the LORD go forth, and fight against those nations, as when he fought in the day of battle. And his feet shall stand in that day upon the mount of Olives, which is before Jerusalem on the east. . . . And the LORD shall be king over all the earth. (Zechariah 14:3-4, 9)

These Scriptures fit in exactly with the message of Jesus. He is revealed in the Gospel as the only Son who has been "pierced," dying by crucifixion, in order to redeem the world, and who will come the second time to judge the world according to how we have responded to His message.

Jesus gave His teaching on His second coming on the Mount of Olives, just outside Jerusalem (Matthew 24, Mark 13, Luke 21), the same place where Zechariah says the Lord is coming in order to save Israel. Jesus ascended into Heaven from the Mount of Olives, and the angel spoke to the disciples saying:

[T]his same Jesus, which is taken up from you into heaven, shall so come in like manner as ye have seen him go into heaven. (Acts 1:11)

The event described in Zechariah, when Israel looks on one who has been pierced, will be the same event as Jesus prophesied concerning Jerusalem at the time of His return, when He said:

Ye shall not see me henceforth, till ye shall say, Blessed is he that cometh in the name of the Lord. (Matthew 23:39)

"Blessed is he that cometh in the name of the Lord" is the welcome for the coming Messiah and indicates that at the end of days Jesus will be welcomed and accepted as Messiah by the Jewish people. Then He will come back to the Earth and finally bring peace to Israel, thus fulfilling the prophecy of Isaiah:

And it shall come to pass in the last days, that the mountain of the LORD's house shall be established in the top of the mountains, and shall be exalted above the hills; and all nations shall flow unto it. And many people shall go and say, Come ye, and let us go up to the mountain of the LORD, to the house of the God of Jacob; and he will teach us of his ways, and we will walk in his paths: for out of Zion shall go forth the law, and the word of the LORD from Jerusalem. And he shall judge among the nations, and shall rebuke many people: and they shall beat their swords into plowshares, and their spears into pruninghooks: nation shall not lift up sword against nation, neither shall they learn war any more. (Isaiah 2:2-4)

In that day, He will fulfill the prophecies of the Reigning King Messiah (Messiah ben David), just as He has already fulfilled the prophecies of the Suffering Servant Messiah (Messiah ben Joseph). Today, He is waiting for the Jewish people to whom He came the first time and whom He continues to love to turn to Him in repentance and faith and recognize He is the real Messiah who came once in humility to be the sacrifice for the sins of the whole world and who is coming again soon in power to judge the world in righteousness according to how we have responded to Him.

WHAT NEXT?

What will happen next is the Messianic Age or Millennium that is described in the Hebrew Prophets and in the prophetic portions of the New Testament. A brief reconstruction of this is as follows:

During the Messianic Age which will follow Jesus' return, God will demonstrate how the Earth should be run. After the devastation caused by the period of trouble which precedes it, living waters will flow out from Jerusalem to clean up the Earth (Zechariah 14:8). Weapons of war will be destroyed, and all military training will cease (Isaiah 2:4, 9:5, Ezekiel 38:9).

The nations will go up to the redeemed Jerusalem where the Messiah will teach them the ways of the Lord (Isaiah 2:2-3). There will be universal peace, and even the animal kingdom will be affected with meat eating creatures becoming vegetarian. The Earth shall be full of the knowledge of the Lord as the waters cover the sea (Isaiah 11:6-9).

This glorious time will be a Sabbath of rest for the Earth. If we take a literal view of creation and reckon the second coming of Messiah to be not too far away, this gives about 6000 years from creation to the end of this age. The Messianic Age or Millennium will last 1000 years according to Revelation. In 2 Peter 3:8, we read that a day with the Lord is as 1000 years. So we have a parallel with the creation account: six days of labor followed by the Sabbath day of rest; 6000 years of travail and sin on the Earth, followed by 1000 years of rest and peace.

Zechariah speaks of the Feast of Tabernacles (Succoth) being celebrated during this time. The Feast of Tabernacles looks back to the time when the Israelites dwelt in booths after they came out of Egypt and before they came into the Promised Land. The booths represent a temporary dwelling place before the final destination, which God has prepared for His people. So the Messianic Age/Millennium is a temporary dwelling place for those who have "come out of Egypt" (symbolizing the world system in rebellion against God) before entering into the final rest in Heaven.

In this time, Messiah will "rule with a rod of iron," but also with absolute justice (Isaiah 11:4-5). The benefits will be obvious to all, especially to those who have experienced the horrors of the great tribulation. Children will be born during this time in the natural way to survivors of the great tribulation who enter the Messianic kingdom. They will not have the opportunity to sin in the way we have today, as Satan will be bound and unable to influence the nations (Revelation 20:1-4).

However, the possibility of sin will be present during this time. In Isaiah, 65:20 we read:

> There shall be no more thence an infant of days, nor an old man that hath not filled his days: for the child shall die an hundred years old; but the sinner being an hundred years old shall be accursed.

We also read of nations that refuse to worship the Lord during this time and suffer judgment as a result (Zechariah 14:17-19). At the end of the thousand-year period, Satan will be loosed for a while and gather together those who are inwardly rebelling against the rule of Messiah:

> And when the thousand years are expired, Satan shall be loosed out of his prison, and shall go out to deceive the nations which are in the four quarters of the earth, Gog and Magog, to gather them together to battle: the number of whom is as the sand of the sea. And they went up on the breadth of the earth, and compassed the camp of the saints about, and the beloved city: and fire came down from God out of heaven, and devoured them. And the devil that deceived them was cast into the lake of fire and brimstone, where the beast and the false prophet are, and shall be tormented day and night for ever and ever. (Revelation 20:7-10)

This will actually be the last battle on Earth, and, like Armageddon, it will end in a moment with Satan's forces being routed. It will also be the end of the world, as Earth and everything in it will be destroyed and the final Day of Judgment before the great white throne of God takes place.

Revelation 19-21 gives a prophetic overview of the events of the end of the world which follows a logical sequence: the battle of Armageddon, the second coming of Messiah to Earth, His rule for 1000 years, Satan's loosing and rebellion at the end of the 1000 years, the end of the world, Heaven and Hell.

After all this, the physical universe in its present form will "melt with fervent heat" and the Earth will be burnt up (2 Peter 3:10). The wicked dead will come before God in judgment:

> And I saw a great white throne, and him that sat on it, from whose face the earth and the heaven fled away; and there was found no place for them. And I saw the dead, small and great, stand before God; and the books were opened: and another book was opened, which is the book of life: and the dead were judged out of those things which were written in the books, according to their works. And the sea gave up the dead which were in it; and death and hell delivered up the dead which were in them: and they were judged every man according to their works. And death and hell were cast into the lake of fire. This is the second death. And whosoever was not found written in the book of life was cast into the lake of fire. (Revelation 20:11-15)

Following this, God will create a new Heaven and a new Earth for those who trust in Jesus as Savior and Lord now. Here, at last, we will experience eternal deliverance from the troubles and pains of this life. Heaven will not end in failure as all the ages of this world have ended in failure because of human sinfulness and satanic activity. Only the Lord will be present there and all those who have been redeemed. Satan and those who have rejected this redemption will be unable to enter.

In the presence of the Lord, the redeemed will have full unbroken fellowship with God such as we can never achieve on Earth because of the weakness of human nature. We will have new bodies that will never get old, sick, or die (1 Corinthians 15). We will also be recognizable to those who have known us and will preserve our identity. Human relationships will not be on the same basis as on Earth. There is no marriage in Heaven, for example (Luke 20:34-36). Because there is no death, there is no need for a new generation to replace the old. But fellowship between the redeemed will be more wonderful than anything we have ever experienced on Earth. The bond of love in Heaven is stronger than the strongest bonds on Earth.

In God's presence is fullness of joy. No one is ever sad in Heaven. None of the things that cause unhappiness on Earth can enter Heaven. There is no unkindness, no cruelty, no selfishness, no loneliness, no misunderstanding.

> And God shall wipe away all tears from their eyes; and there shall be no more death, neither sorrow, nor crying, neither shall there be any more pain: for the former things are passed away. (Revelation 21:4)

Make sure you are going there by accepting the salvation offered us all by the Messiah Jesus who is King of Kings and Lord of Lords. Amen.

> The time is fulfilled, and the kingdom of God is at hand: repent ye, and believe the gospel. (Mark 1:15)

Appendix

MESSIANIC PROPHECIES FULFILLED AND AS YET UNFULFILLED

PROPHECIES OF THE FIRST COMING OF MESSIAH

MESSIAH TO BE BORN IN BETHLEHEM

Prophecy

> But thou, Bethlehem Ephratah, though thou be little among the thousands of Judah, yet out of thee shall he come forth unto me that is to be ruler in Israel; whose goings forth have been from of old, from everlasting. (Micah 5:2; 5:1 in Jewish Bibles)

Fulfillment

> And when he [Herod] had gathered all the chief priests and scribes of the people together, he demanded of them where Christ should be born. And they said unto him, In Bethlehem of Judæa: for thus it is written by the prophet. (Matthew 2:4-5; for whole quote see Matthew 2:1-6 and Luke 2:1-20)

MESSIAH TO BE BORN OF A VIRGIN

Prophecy

Therefore the Lord himself shall give you a sign; Behold, a virgin shall conceive, and bear a son, and shall call his name Immanuel. (Isaiah 7:14)

Fulfillment

Now the birth of Jesus Christ was on this wise: When as his mother Mary was espoused to Joseph, before they came together, she was found with child of the Holy Ghost . . . the angel of the Lord appeared unto him [Joseph] in a dream, saying, Joseph, thou son of David, fear not to take unto thee Mary thy wife: for that which is conceived in her is of the Holy Ghost. And she shall bring forth a son, and thou shalt call his name JESUS [Yeshua in Hebrew, meaning salvation]: for he shall save his people from their sins. (Matthew 1:18-21; for whole quote see Matthew 1:18-25)

MESSIAH TO BE A SON WHO IS ALSO THE MIGHTY GOD

Prophecy

For unto us a child is born, unto us a son is given: and the government shall be upon his shoulder: and his name shall be called Wonderful, Counsellor, The mighty God, The everlasting Father, The Prince of Peace. (Isaiah 9:6)

Fulfillment

The Holy Ghost shall come upon thee [Mary], and the power of the Highest shall overshadow thee: therefore also that holy thing which shall be born of thee shall be called the Son of God. (Luke 1:35)

MESSIAH TO PREACH THE GOOD NEWS WITH A MINISTRY OF MIRACLES

Prophecy

The Spirit of the Lord God is upon me; because the LORD hath anointed me to preach good tidings unto the meek; he hath sent me to bind up the brokenhearted, to proclaim liberty to the captives, and the opening of the prison to them that are bound. (Isaiah 61:1)

Fulfillment

And Jesus went about all the cities and villages, teaching in their synagogues, and preaching the gospel of the kingdom, and healing every sickness and every disease among the people. (Matthew 9:35)

MESSIAH TO TEACH IN PARABLES

Prophecy

I will open my mouth in a parable. (Psalm 78:2)

Fulfillment

All these things spake Jesus unto the multitude in parables; and without a parable spake he not unto them. (Matthew 13:34)

MESSIAH TO BE A LIGHT TO THE GENTILES

Prophecy

I will also give thee for a light to the Gentiles, that thou mayest be my salvation unto the end of the earth. (Isaiah 49:6)

Fulfillment

[F]or mine eyes have seen thy salvation, which thou hast prepared before the face of all people; a light to lighten the Gentiles, and the glory of thy people Israel. (Luke 2:30-32; see also Matthew 28:18-20 and Acts 13:47-48)

MESSIAH TO ENTER JERUSALEM ON A DONKEY

Prophecy

Rejoice greatly, O daughter of Zion; shout, O daughter of Jerusalem: behold, thy King cometh unto thee: he is just, and having salvation; lowly, and riding upon an ass, and upon a colt the foal of an ass. (Zechariah 9:9)

Fulfillment

. . . and brought the ass, and the colt, and put on them their clothes, and they set him thereon. And a very great multitude spread their garments in the way; others cut down branches from the trees, and strawed them in the way. (Matthew 21:7-8)

THE MESSIANIC GREETING TO BE GIVEN MESSIAH ON THIS OCCASION

Prophecy

This is the day which the LORD hath made; we will rejoice and be glad in it. Save now, I beseech thee, O LORD [Hebrew "hoshia na"/Greek hosanna]: O LORD, I beseech thee, send now prosperity. Blessed be he that cometh in the name of the LORD: we have blessed you out of the house of the LORD. (Psalm 118:24-26)

Fulfillment

And the multitudes that went before, and that followed, cried, saying, Hosanna [Hebrew hoshia na] to the Son of David: Blessed is he that cometh in the name of the Lord. (Matthew 21:9)

DESPITE TRIUMPHAL ENTRY, MESSIAH ENTERED JERUSALEM TO BE REJECTED AND SACRIFICED

Prophecy

The stone which the builders refused is become the head stone of the corner . . . bind the sacrifice with cords, even unto the horns of the altar.(Psalm 118:22, 27)

Fulfillment

From that time forth began Jesus to shew unto his disciples, how that he must go unto Jerusalem, and suffer many things of the elders and chief priests and scribes, and be killed, and be raised again the third day. (Matthew 16:21)

MESSIAH TO BE BETRAYED FOR 30 PIECES OF SILVER

Prophecy

So they weighed for my price thirty pieces of silver. And the LORD said unto me, Cast it unto the potter: a goodly price that I was prised at of them. And I took the thirty pieces of silver, and cast them to the potter in the house of the LORD. (Zechariah 11:12-13)

Fulfillment

Then one of the twelve, called Judas Iscariot, went unto the chief priests, and said unto them, What will ye give me, and I will deliver him unto you? And they covenanted with him for thirty pieces of silver. (Matthew 26:14-15; see also Matthew 27:3-10)

MESSIAH TO BE FORSAKEN BY HIS DISCIPLES

Prophecy

Awake, O sword, against my shepherd, and against the man that is my fellow, saith the LORD of hosts: smite the shepherd, and the sheep shall be scattered. (Zechariah 13:7)

Fulfillment

And they all forsook him, and fled. (Mark 14:50)

MESSIAH TO BE DUMB BEFORE HIS ACCUSERS

Prophecy

He was oppressed, and he was afflicted, yet he opened not his mouth. (Isaiah 53:7)

Fulfillment

And when he was accused of the chief priests and elders, he answered nothing. (Matthew 27:12)

MESSIAH TO BE SMITTEN AND SPAT UPON

Prophecy

I gave my back to the smiters, and my cheeks to them that plucked off the hair: I hid not my face from shame and spitting. (Isaiah 50:6)

Fulfillment

Then did they spit in his face, and buffeted him; and others smote him with the palms of their hands. (Matthew 26:67)

MESSIAH TO BE MOCKED

Prophecy

All they that see me laugh me to scorn: they shoot out the lip, they shake the head, saying, He trusted on the LORD that he would deliver him: let him deliver him, seeing he delighted in him. (Psalm 22:7-8)

Fulfillment

Likewise also the chief priests mocking him, with the scribes and elders, said, He saved others; himself he cannot save. If he be the King of Israel, let him now come down from the cross, and we will believe him. He trusted in God; let him deliver him now, if he will have him. (Matthew 27:41-43)

MESSIAH TO HAVE HIS HANDS AND FEET PIERCED

Prophecy

[T]hey pierced my hands and my feet. (Psalm 22:16)

[A]nd they shall look upon me whom they have pierced. (Zechariah 12:10)

Fulfillment

And when they were come to the place, which is called Calvary, there they crucified him. (Luke 23:33)

MESSIAH TO BE PUT TO DEATH WITH CRIMINALS

Prophecy

[H]e was numbered with the transgressors. (Isaiah 53:12)

Fulfillment

Then were there two thieves crucified with him, one on the right hand, and another on the left. (Matthew 27:38)

MESSIAH TO MAKE INTERCESSION FOR HIS PERSECUTORS

Prophecy

[H]e bare the sin of many, and made intercession for the transgressors. (Isaiah 53:12)

Fulfillment

Then said Jesus, Father, forgive them; for they know not what they do. (Luke 23:34)

MESSIAH'S BONES NOT TO BE BROKEN

Prophecy

He keepeth all his bones: not one of them is broken. (Psalm 34:20; see also Exodus 12:46, Numbers 9:22)

Fulfillment

But when they came to Jesus, and saw that he was dead already, they brake not his legs . . . For these things were done, that the scripture should be fulfilled, A bone of him shall not be broken. (John 19:33, 36)

MESSIAH TO BE BURIED IN A RICH MAN'S TOMB

Prophecy

And he made his grave with the wicked, and with the rich in his death. (Isaiah 53:9)

Fulfillment

When the even was come, there came a rich man of Arimathæa, named Joseph, who also himself was Jesus' disciple: he went to Pilate, and begged the body of Jesus. Then Pilate commanded the body to be delivered. And when Joseph had taken the body, he wrapped it in a clean linen cloth, and laid it in his own new tomb, which he had hewn out in the rock: and he rolled a great stone to the door of the sepulchre, and departed. (Matthew 27:57-60)

MESSIAH TO RISE AGAIN FROM THE DEAD

Prophecy

For thou wilt not leave my soul in hell (Sheol, the place of the dead); neither wilt thou suffer thine Holy One to see corruption. Thou wilt shew me the path of life. (Psalm 16:10-11)

[F]or he was cut off out of the land of the living . . . when thou shalt make his soul an offering for sin, he shall see his seed, he shall prolong his days. (Isaiah 53:8, 10)

Fulfillment

Why seek ye the living among the dead? He is not here, but is risen. (Luke 24:5-6)

THE MESSAGE OF SALVATION THROUGH MESSIAH TO GO INTO ALL THE WORLD

Prophecy

Look unto me, and be ye saved, all the ends of the earth: for I am God, and there is none else. I have sworn by myself, the word is gone out of my mouth in righteousness, and shall not return, That unto me every knee shall bow. (Isaiah 45:22-23)

Fulfillment

And Jesus came and spake unto them, saying, All power is given unto me in heaven and in earth. Go ye therefore, and teach all nations, baptizing them in the name of the Father, and of the Son, and of the Holy Ghost: teaching them to observe all things whatsoever I have commanded you: and, lo, I am with you alway, even unto the end of the world. (Matthew 28:18-20)

PROPHECIES OF THE SECOND COMING OF MESSIAH

A TIME OF UNPARALLELED TROUBLE TO PRECEDE THE DAY OF THE LORD

Prophecy

And at that time shall Michael stand up, the great prince which standeth for the children of thy people: and there shall be a time of trouble, such as never was since there was a nation even to that same time. (Daniel 12:1)

New Testament parallel

[F]or then shall be great tribulation, such as was not since the beginning of the world to this time, no, nor ever shall be. (Matthew 24:21)

FOCAL POINT OF THIS TIME OF TROUBLE TO BE JERUSALEM

Prophecy

And in that day will I make Jerusalem a burdensome stone for all people: all that burden themselves with it shall be cut in pieces, though all the people of the earth be gathered together against it. (Zechariah 12:3)

New Testament parallel

And when ye shall see Jerusalem compassed with armies, then know that the desolation thereof is nigh. . . . Jerusalem shall be trodden down of the Gentiles, until the times of the Gentiles be fulfilled. (Luke 21:20, 24)

ALL NATIONS TO BE GATHERED FOR THE FINAL BATTLE

Prophecy

Assemble yourselves, and come, all ye heathen, and gather yourselves together round about: thither cause thy mighty ones to come down, O LORD. Let the heathen be wakened, and come up to the valley of Jehoshaphat [Hebrew word means "The Lord judges"]. (Joel 3:11-12)

New Testament parallel

For they are the spirits of devils, working miracles, which go forth unto the kings of the earth and of the whole world, to gather them to the battle of that great day of God Almighty. And he gathered them together into a place called in the Hebrew tongue Armageddon. (Revelation 16:14, 16)

MESSIAH TO COME IN THE CLOUDS OF HEAVEN

Prophecy

I saw in the night visions, and, behold, one like the Son of man came with the clouds of heaven. (Daniel 7:13)

New Testament parallel

[A]nd then shall appear the sign of the Son of man in heaven: and then shall all the tribes of the earth mourn, and they shall see the Son of man coming in the clouds of heaven with power and great glory. (Matthew 24:30)

MESSIAH TO BE VISIBLE AS ONE WHO HAS BEEN PIERCED

Prophecy

And I will pour upon the house of David, and upon the inhabitants of Jerusalem, the spirit of grace and of supplications: and they shall look upon me whom they have pierced, and they shall mourn for him, as one mourneth for his only son. (Zechariah 12:10)

New Testament parallel

Behold, he cometh with clouds; and every eye shall see him, and they also which pierced him: and all kindreds of the earth shall wail because of him. (Revelation 1:7)

MESSIAH TO COME TO THE MOUNT OF OLIVES

Prophecy

Then shall the LORD go forth, and fight against those nations, as when he fought in the day of battle. And his feet shall stand in that day upon the mount of Olives, which is before Jerusalem on the east. (Zechariah 14:3-4)

New Testament parallel

Ye men of Galilee, why stand ye gazing up into heaven? this same Jesus, which is taken up from you into heaven, shall so come in like manner as ye have seen him go into heaven. Then returned they unto Jerusalem from the mount called Olivet. (Acts 1:11-12)

MESSIAH TO COME WITH THE SAINTS

Prophecy

[A]nd the LORD my God shall come, and all the saints with thee. (Zechariah 14:5)

New Testament parallel

Behold, the Lord cometh with ten thousands of his saints. (Jude 14; "saints" in the Bible means all who truly believe in the Lord)

THE WICKED TO FLEE FROM THE COMING OF THE LORD

Prophecy

In that day a man shall cast his idols . . . to go into the clefts of the rocks, and into the tops of the ragged rocks, for fear of the LORD, and for the glory of his majesty, when he ariseth to shake terribly the earth. (Isaiah 2:20-21)

New Testament parallel

And the kings of the earth, and the great men, and the rich men, and the chief captains, and the mighty men, and every bondman, and every free man, hid themselves in the dens and in the rocks of the mountains; and said to the mountains and rocks, Fall on us, and hide us from the face of him that sitteth on the throne, and from the wrath of the Lamb. (Revelation 6:15-16)

THE LORD TO ESTABLISH RIGHTEOUSNESS AND PEACE ON THE EARTH. SATAN TO BE UNABLE TO DECEIVE THE NATIONS

Prophecy

And it shall come to pass in the last days, that the mountain of the LORD'S house shall be established in the top of the mountains, and shall be exalted above the hills; and all nations shall flow unto it. And many people shall go and say, Come ye, and let us go up to the mountain of the LORD, to the house of the God of Jacob; and he will teach us of his ways, and we will walk in his paths: for out of Zion shall go forth the law, and the word of the LORD from Jerusalem. And he shall judge among the nations, and shall rebuke many people: and they shall beat their swords into plowshares, and their spears into pruninghooks: nation shall not lift up sword against nation, neither shall they learn war any more. (Isaiah 2:2-4)

New Testament parallel

And I saw an angel come down from heaven, having the key of the bottomless pit and a great chain in his hand. And he laid hold on the dragon, that old serpent, which is the Devil, and Satan, and bound him a thousand years . . . that he should deceive the nations no more . . . Blessed and holy is he that hath part in the first resurrection: on such the second death hath no power, but they shall be priests of God and of Christ, and shall reign with him a thousand years. (Revelation 20:1-3, 6; extracts)

ISRAEL TO BE SAVED AND BLESSED OF THE LORD IN THE MIDST OF THE NATIONS

Prophecy

In that day shall Israel be the third with Egypt and with Assyria, even a blessing in the midst of the land: whom the LORD of hosts shall bless, saying, Blessed be Egypt my people, and Assyria the work of my hands, and Israel mine inheritance. (Isaiah 19:24-25)

New Testament parallel

And so all Israel shall be saved: as it is written, There shall come out of Sion the Deliverer, and shall turn away ungodliness from Jacob: for this is my covenant unto them, when I shall take away their sins. (Romans 11:26-27)

FOLLOWING THE MILLENNIAL REIGN OF MESSIAH ON EARTH, GOD TO CREATE NEW HEAVENS AND A NEW EARTH

Prophecy

For as the new heavens and the new earth, which I will make, shall remain before me, saith the LORD, so shall your seed and your name remain. (Isaiah 66:22)

New Testament parallel

And I saw a new heaven and a new earth: for the first heaven and the first earth were passed away; . . . And I heard a great voice out of heaven saying, Behold, the tabernacle of God is with men, and he will dwell with them, and they shall be his people, and God himself shall be with them, and be their God. (Revelation 21:1-3; extracts)

ENDNOTES:

Chapter 2: Who Killed Jesus?

1. John Chrysostom (c. 349-407), author of "Homilae Adversus Iudaeos" ("Homilies Against the Jews") was the Archbishop of Constantinople. His anti-Semitic writings have influenced many over the centuries.

2. Pope Innocent III, "Letter to the Count of Nevers" (1209); cited in Solomon Grayzel's *The Church and the Jews in the XIIIth Century: A study of their relations during the years 1198-1254, based on the papal letters and the conciliar decrees of the period* (New York, NY: Hermon Press, revised edition, 1966), p. 127.

3. Martin Luther (1483-1546), who wrote *Concerning the Jews and Their Lies*, was a key figure in the German Reformation.

Chapter 3: Out of Night

1. Elie Wiesel, *Night* (New York, NY: Bantam books, 1982 edition), pp. 30-32.

2. Ibid., p. 64.

3. Elie Wiesel, *Night* (Hill and Wang, 1959, First Edition), Foreword, pp. 7-8.

4. Friedrich Nietzsche, *The Antichrist* (1990 Penguin edition which includes both *Twilight of Idols* and *Anti-Christ*; 2003 printing; Kindle version), p. 140.

5. Ibid., p. .140.

6. Ibid., p. 127.

7. Ibid., p. 130.

8. Louis L. Snyder, *Hitler and Nazism* (New York, NY: Bantam Doubleday Dell Publishing Group, Bantam Edition, 1967), p. 87.

9. Ibid., p. 90.

10. Ibid., p. 91.

11. André Schwartz-Bart, *The Last of the Just* (New York, NY: The Overlook Press, U.S.A. Edition, 2000; first published in 1960), pp. 157, 159.

12. Baal Shem Tov—"Master of the Good Name," the title given to Israel ben Eliezer (1698-1760), the founder of the Hasidim movement.

13. Andre Schwartz-Bart, *The Last of the Just*, op. cit., p. 213.

14. Ibid., p. 213.

Chapter 4: So What About the Messiah?

1. Prayer quoted in *Atlas of Jewish History* by Martin Gilbert (Dorset Press, Third Edition, 1985), p. 53.

2. Lubavitch is a Hassidic Jewish Orthodox movement which has been very active in promoting the hope of the coming Messiah under the influence of

its late leader, Rabbi Menachem Schneerson, also known as The Lubavitcher Rebbe. When he died in 1994, some of his followers put forward the view that he himself was the Messiah and that he would return (i.e. rise again from the dead!). This view is a minority view and is strongly contested by mainstream opinion in Judaism today.

3. Maimonides Hilchos Melachim 11:1 and 4 from the Mishneh Torah. Taken from The Laws concerning Mashiach produced by Lubavitch.

4. Ibid.

5. This section is taken from a section of Maimonides' Mishneh Torah (Hilchos Melachim 11:4) which was deleted from most of the editions published since the Venice edition of 1574 as a result of censorship by the Roman Catholic Church.

6. "Ask the Rabbi" column from the *Jewish Chronicle*.

7. Lubavitch is active in reaching out to Jewish people on the streets of Jewish areas and passes out leaflets about their beliefs from their headquarters in Stamford Hill, London. These quotations are taken from such leaflets.

8. Advertisement in the *Jerusalem Post* (31/8/91).

9. Rabbi Meir Simcha Sokolovsky, *Prophecy and Providence: The Fulfillment of Torah Prophecies in the Course of Jewish History* (Nanuet, NY: Feldheim Publishers, First Edition, September 1991), p. 197.

10. Ibid., p. 195.

11. Ibid., p. 193.

12. Ibid., .p 191.

13. Sanhedrin 98a.

14. Ibid.

Chapter 5: Messiah—A Great Man or a Divine Person?

1. Aryeh Kaplan, *The Real Messiah: A Jewish Response to Missionaries*, (New York, NY: OUNCSY Publications, New Edition, 1985, eleventh printing 2013), p. 27.

2. David Berger, *The Rebbe, the Messiah and the Scandal of Orthodox Indifference* (The Littman Library of Jewish Civilization, 1st edition, September 1, 2001), p. 14.

3. Used with permission from Messianic Vision.

4. Exodus 23:19: "You shall not boil a young goat in its mother's milk" is interpreted by rabbinic Judaism to mean that you should not eat milk and meat in the same meal.

5. The name of God is considered too holy to pronounce and is therefore spoken as "Adonai," meaning the Lord, in Jewish worship. It is not known how the four letters of God's name recorded in the Bible should be pronounced. Modern variations are Jehovah and Yahweh.

6. Sohar, Gen. versa (Amsterdam Edition) p. 15.

7. Hirsch Prinz (aka: Christian William Henry Pauli and Tzvi Nassi), *The Great Mystery: How Can Three Be One?* (Yanetz Ltd., 2nd edition, 1974; man-

uscript online at: https://play.google.com/books/reader?id=UYkEAAAAQA-AJ&printsec=frontcover&output=reader&hl=en&pg=GBS.PR1), pp. 27-28.

8. Ibid., p. 32.

9. Ibid., p. 56.

10. Ibid., p 58.

11. Ibid., p. 57-60.

12. Ibid., p 61.

13. Ibid.

14. Ibid., p. 85; quoting "Tikunei Ha Zohar" cap. 67, page 130.

Chapter 6: Can We Believe in the Virgin Birth?

1. Debate put on by London L'Chaim Society January 19, 1998.

2. Arnold Fruchtenbaum, *Messianic Christology* (San Antonio, TX: Ariel Ministries, June 1, 1998), pp. 35-37.

3. Ibid., pp. 36-37.

4. Jerusalem Talmud, Chagigah 2:4, Sanhedrin 23:3, Babylonian Talmud, Sanhedrin 44:2.

Chapter 7: The Suffering Servant

1. Arnold Fruchtenbaum, *Messianic Christology,* op. cit., p. 54.

2. A.D. Neubauer and S.R. Driver, *The Fifty-Third Chapter of Isaiah According to the Jewish Interpreters* (Skokie,IL: Varda Books, 2005), p. 5.

3. Dr. A. Th. Philips, *Prayer Book for the Day of Atonement* (New York, NY: Hebrew Publishing Company, 1931) p. 239.

4. *The Fifty-Third Chapter of Isaiah According to the Jewish Interpreters,* op. cit., pp. lxiii, 114.

5. Ibid., p. 258.

6. Ibid., p. 386.

Chapter 8: "When I See the Blood"

1. Berachot 55a.

2. Berachot 12b.

3. Moses Maimonides, Mishneh Torah, Laws of Repentance, 1:3, 2.1, 9-10.

Chapter 9: The Fall of the Second Temple

1. The Temple Mount Faithful is a religious Zionist movement that believes the Jewish Temple should be rebuilt on its ancient site, now occupied by the Muslim Dome of the Rock Mosque. Followers are preparing vessels to be used in the rebuilt Temple and are training men of the priestly line (Cohens) to offer the animal sacrifices.

2. The Menorah is the seven-branched candlestick placed in the Tabernacle in the Wilderness and in the Temple. When the Romans destroyed the Temple in 70 AD, they took its treasures to Rome in triumph. The Arch of Titus in

Rome depicts the Menorah being carried off.

3. Rabbi Ken Spiro, "Crash Course in Jewish History Part 35—Destruction of the Temple" (http://www.aish.com/jl/h/cc/48944036.html).

4. Mitch and Zhava Glaser, *The Fall Feasts of Israel* (Chicago, IL: Moody Press, 1987, Kindle edition), Kindle location 1585-1610.

5. Ibid., Kindle location 1595.

6. Rachmiel Frydland, *When Being Jewish Was a Crime* (Messianic Publishing Co., 2nd edition, 1998), pp. 71-73.

Chapter 10: No Peace—No Messiah

1. Aryeh Kaplan, *The Real Messiah?*, op. cit., p. 71.

2. *Operation Judaism Fact Pack* compiled by Rabbi S Arkush; pp. 13-15.

3. Rabbi Alshech lived in Safed in Upper Galilee in the second half of the 16th century. This passage is quoted in *The Suffering Servant of Isaiah According to the Jewish Interpretations* by Samuel R. Driver and Adolf Neubauer (New York, NY: Hermon Press,1877, Reprint 1969), p. 258.

4. David Baron, *Visions and Prophecies of Zechariah* (Originally published by Morgan & Scott, LTD, 1918, Kindle edition), p. 329, Kindle location 6414.

5. Ibid., p. 328, Kindle location 6404. David Baron (1855-1926) was a notable Hebrew Christian who founded the Hebrew Christian Testimony to Israel in 1893 and was the author of a number of books, showing the significance of Messianic prophecy and its fulfilment in Jesus the Messiah. These include *Rays of Messiah's Glory, Types, Psalms and Prophecies*, and *Visions and Prophecies of Zechariah*.

6. Sukkot 52a.

7. Sanhedrin 98a.

8. See endnote #7, chapter four.

9. Rabbi Arye Forta in L'Eylah, "The New Christian Missions to the Jews—How should we respond?" (*A Journal of Judaism Today*, published by the Office of the Chief Rabbi, Issue 25), p. 22.

10. Rachmiel Frydland, "Rabbis Speak About Messiah" (Zion Messianic Fellowship, http://www.zmf.org/teachings/?action=articles&article=Rabbis%20Speak%20About%20Messiah).

Chapter 11: Is Torah the Bridge to God?

1. Torah in Judaism means more than just the five books of Moses that make up the Pentateuch in the Bible. The word literally means "teaching" rather than "law," and it has come to mean the whole of Jewish teaching to be found in the Written and the Oral Torah. According to Rabbi Louis Jacobs, this includes "the later applications and deeper understanding of these down to the present day, so that Torah is synonymous with the Jewish religion"; quoted from *The Jewish Religion—a Companion*, p. 562.

2. Emanuel Feldman, *On Judaism: Conversations on Being Jewish in Today's World* (Brooklyn, NY: Shaar Press, 1994, Third Impression, 2003), p. 103.

3. Rabbi Simmons, "ABCs of Shavuot" (http://www.aish.com/h/sh/t/48959111.html?s=srcon).

4. Rabbi Simmons, "Necessity of Oral Law" (Aish ha Torah's Discovery Seminar, http://www.aish.com/atr/Necessity_of_Oral_Law.html).

5. Rabbi Kaplan, "The Oral Tradition" (Aish website: http://www.aish.com/jl/b/ol/48943186.html).

6. The 613 Commandments (Aish website: http://www.aish.com/h/sh/se/48945081.html?s=srcon).

7. Dr. Daniel Grubner, "Objections Based on Traditional Judaism"

8. Rabbi Dr. I. Epstein, editor, *The Babylonian Talmud* (London: Soncino Press, 1935), Aboth I,1 n.7 Cf. Pes. 2b, Er.100b, and Sanh.46a.

9. "A Fence Around the Torah" (http://www.elijahnet.net/A%20FENCE%20AROUND%20THE%20TORAH.html), ciiting Pesachim 2b.

10. Rabbi Gil Student, "The Oral Law" (2001, http://www.aishdas.org/student/oral.htm).

11. Herbert Danby, *The Mishnah: Translated from the Hebrew with Introduction and Brief Explanatory Notes* (Peabody, MA: Hendrickson Publishers, 1933, First Hendrickson Softcover Edition, November 2011), p. 106.

12. Antiquities 13: 297.

13. Albert Baumgarten, "The Pharisaic Paradosis" (*Harvard Theological Review*, 1987, http://www.jstor.org/stable/1509655), p 63.

14. Rabbi Aryeh Kaplan, *The Handbook of Jewish Thought* (Moznaim Pub. Corp., 1st edition, June 1, 1990); taken from http://www.aish.com/jl/m/pm/48936762.html.

15. Rabbi Arian, "Rabban Yohanan ben Zakkai and the New Paradigm" (December 29, 2011, http://rabbiarian.blogspot.co.uk/2011/12/rabban-yohanan-ben.html).

16. Arnold Fruchtenbaum, "The Law of Moses and the Law of Messiah" (*Ariel Ministries Digital Press*, MBS 006, http://www.arielm.org/dcs/pdf/mbs006m.pdf), pp. 8-12.

Chapter 12: The Messiah and the End of Days

1. Rabbi Pinchas Winston, "Moshiach and the World Today" (Aish website, June 23, 2001, http://www.aish.com/jw/s/48883092.html).

2. Mark Twain, *The Innocents Abroad* (1869, public domain), pp. 273-274.

3. President Rivlin addresses opening of the Winter Session of the 20th Knesset (Israel Ministry of Foreign Affairs, October 12, 2015, http://mfa.gov.il/MFA/PressRoom/2015/Pages/President-Rivlin-addresses-the-opening-of-the-Winter-Session-of-the-20th-Knesset-12-October-2015.aspx).

4. Adam Eliyahu Berkowitz, "Prominent Rabbis Sternbuch, Amar Hint

that the Messiah is 'Just Around the Corner'" (*Breaking Israel News,* December 9, 2015, https://www.breakingisraelnews.com/55777/turkeysyria-conflict-unfolding-prominent-rabbis-hint-messiah-around-corner-jewish-world/#xl8oX-f5ubvpOdrkT.99).

5. https://israel365.com/store.

6. Rabbi Pinchas Winston, *Survival Guide for the End of Days* (https://www.israel365.com/2015/06/survival-guide-for-the-end-of-days/).

7. https://www.israel365.com/store/books/not-just-another-scenario-2/#ZHiC3x7ckMBAQ1tF.99.

8. Dr. Rivkah Lambert Adler, "Do Putin's Actions in Syria Fulfill the Prophecy of Ezekiel Regarding Gog and Magog?" (*Breaking Israel News,* October 14, 2015, https://www.breakingisraelnews.com/51078/do-putins-actions-in-syria-fulfill-the-prophecy-of-ezekiel-regarding-gog-and-magog-middle-east/#70u484GA1MgDWD1V.99).

9. Roy Neuberger, *Working Towards Moshiach* (Messiah) (Philipp Feldheim, September 1, 2015); taken from the book description: https://www.israel365.com/store/books/working-toward-moshiach).

10. Jerusalem Post staff, "Abbas Gives Victory Speech in Ramallah: "We have a state now." (*Jerusalem Post*, December 2, 2012, http://www.jpost.com/printarticle.aspx?id=294280).

11. Aryeh Kaplan, *The Real Messiah?*, op. cit., p. 83.

12. Ibid., p. 83.

13. Ibid., p. 89; taken from *Netzach Yisroel* No. 36. Cf. *Sanhedrin* 98b and Cf. *Emunos VeDeyos* 8:6.

14. Ibid., p. 91, citing *Yad,Melachim* 11:3, *Yeshuos Meshicho* No.3, p.45 ff., *Lekutey Tshuvos Chasam Sofer* No.98.

15. Ibid., p. 91.

16. Ibid., p. 92.

17. Ibid.

18. Ibid., p. 95.

PHOTO CREDITS

Cover/page 3 photo: From bigstockphoto.com; used with permission; cover design by Light for the Last Days

Page 8: Public domain.

Page 12: Orthodox Jews dancing at Western Wall in Jerusalem in 2015; from bigstockphoto.com; used with permission.

Page 26: Both photos from United States Holocaust Memorial Museum; used with permission.

Page 46: Photo from bigstockphoto.com; used with permission.

Page 54: By Raphael, "Prophet Abraham and the Three Angels"; public domain.

Index

A

Abraham 17, 19, 53-56, 60, 67, 71, 76, 102, 107, 113-114, 133
Adam and Eve 53, 71, 102
age of peace 121, 130, 138
Ahaz 67, 70, 73-78, 82
Akiba, Rabbi 115
Allen, Sharon 50
Al-Qaeda 10
Alshech, Rabbi 86, 97, 124, 125
Amar, Rabbi 164
America
ancient pagan religions 132
Andre Schwartz-Bart 34
Angel
 of Death 105, 114
 of God 61, 62
 of the Covenant 60, 61
 of the Lord 51, 56-57, 59, 61, 136
animal sacrifices 91, 99, 101, 106-109, 116, 118
antichrist 14, 27, 32, 170-172
anti-Jewish laws 14
Antiochus Epiphanes 171
anti-Semitism 13, 16, 24, 35, 87-88
Arab-Israeli conflict 164, 166, 170
Arab Muslim nations 167, 172
Arkush, Rabbi S. 122-123, 128-129

Armageddon 164, 172, 178
Assyria 73, 74
Assyrian
 Empire 76
 invasion 76
 Assyrians 72, 75, 76, 78
atheism 31
atonement 35, 98-103, 106-107, 118, 123-125, 153, 157
Auschwitz 25, 26, 27, 28
 also see Holocaust

B

Babel 133
Babylonian
 Empire 76, 113
 exile 101
 Talmud 144
Bar Cochba 115
Baron, David 124
Bechai, Rabbi 61, 62
Beit Ha Mikdash 38
Berger, Rabbi David 48
Bethlehem 49, 92, 138
Birkenau 26, 27, 28
blood of bulls and of goats 91, 99, 104, 157
Boteach, Rabbi Shmuley 65-66, 68-70
British Israelism 75
Buddhism 131

Because of the frequency of their use, certain words (such as Israel, Torah, Jerusalem, etc.) are not included in this index.

C

Caesarea Philippi 9, 10
Chrysostom, John 13
communion 127
Communism 43, 138
Constantine 14
Council of Nicea 14
Crispin, Rabbi Moshe
Cohen Ibn 86
crucifixion 17, 18, 20, 78,
89, 95, 114, 115, 167, 174

D

David Ben Gurion 164
Day of Atonement 85,
116, 117, 157
Day of Judgment 160, 178
Day of Pentecost 90
destruction of the Temple
104, 106, 110-112, 116-
118, 138, 149, 153, 171
Diaspora 158
disciples 9, 17, 22, 92, 95,
96, 105, 107, 133, 135-
136, 150, 156, 174
Dome of the Rock mosque 109
Dosa, Rabbi 125

E

Eliyahu de Vidas, Rabbi 86, 88
end of days 40, 42-43,
57, 164, 166, 173, 175
environmental destruction 41
EU 170, 171

F

false peace covenant 171, 172
Feast of Tabernacles 176

festival of Shavuoth 142
Fiddler on the Roof 15
Final Solution 16
first Crusade in 1096 14
forced baptism 15
Forta, Rabbi Arye 131
free-will 136
French Revolution 30
Fruchtenbaum, Arnold
77, 79, 85, 154, 155
Frydland, Rachmiel 118, 119

G

German Faith Movement 33
Gethsemane 10, 19
Glaser, Mitch 116
Gog and Magog 165, 177
great tribulation 135, 177
Grubner, Dr. Dan 146

H

Hanasi, Rabbi Judah 144
Hebrew Bible 42, 51, 60, 63, 151
Hinduism 131
Hitler, Adolph 27, 32, 33, 168
Holocaust 10, 16, 26, 29,
30, 31, 34, 88, 119
Holy of Holies 116, 157
Holy Spirit 10, 24, 42, 60, 80,
82, 120, 135, 153, 160, 166
House of David 38, 78

I

interfaith religious circles 131
Islam 10, 60, 131
Israeli-Palestinian conflict
    see Arab-Israeli conflict

J

Jewish
Bible 22, 42, 51-52, 58-59, 122
Messiah 22, 48, 65
State 165
Jihad 164
Jonathan ben Uzziel 61, 85
Josephus 148
judgment 34, 50, 68, 84, 104, 107-108, 122, 128-130, 138, 146, 158, 167, 177-178

K

Kalir, Rabbi Eliezer 85, 88
Kaplan, Rabbi Aryeh 47, 65, 121, 144, 152, 168-170
kingdom of God 82, 96, 105, 135, 179
King Edward I 15
King Hezekiah, 50, 82

L

Land of Israel Faithful Movement 109
latter days 166
Lebanon 9, 85, 117
Levi, Rabbi Yehoshua ben 126
Levy, Ernie 34, 36
Liberal Christian scholarship 66
lkveta d'Meshicha 44
Lord's Supper 127
Lubavitch 43, 48, 130
Lubavitcher Rebbe 37
Lubavitch movement 43, 48
Luther, Martin 15

M

Mahmoud Abbas 167
Maimonides 38, 42, 85, 101
Malamud, Bernard 24
Marxism 40
Mary 79, 80
Melchizedek 107
Messianic
Age 168, 176
kingdom 129, 137, 168, 177
line 71, 73, 78
prophecies 44, 123, 127, 128, 138
prophecy 57, 71, 75
Middle East 131, 161, 162, 169, 170
Mishna, the 117, 144
mitzvoth 38, 39
modern Judaism 38, 42, 100, 104, 130, 149, 157, 158
Moses 38, 61-62, 96, 99, 102-103, 110-112, 140, 142, 143-146, 148-151, 154-155, 158-159
Moses Maimonides 38
Moshiach ben David 44
Moshiach ben Yoseph 44
Mount of Olives 57, 58, 114, 139, 167, 174
Mount Sinai 141, 142, 143, 146
Muslims 11, 14, 66, 166

N

Nachman, Rabbi Moses ben 61
Nathan, Rabbi 100
Nazis/Nazism 15, 16, 27-29-33, 34-35
Nebuchadnezzar 58

new birth 135, 160
New Covenant 19, 104-106, 113-114, 150, 154-155, 158-159
Nietzsche, Friedrich 30-31
1948 163, 164, 166
Noah 41, 71, 102

O

Oakland, Roger 80
Old Covenant 105
Oral Law 38, 144, 146, 150, 152
Oral Torah 142-147, 149, 151
Orthodox Jews/Judaism 10, 12, 16, 43, 47, 50, 57-58, 66, 109, 152-153

P

paganism 33
pagan worship 132
Palestine 14, 163, 167
Palestinian Authority 167
Palestinians 167
Palestinian state 166, 167
Panitz, Rabbi David 35
Passover 15, 103, 104, 105, 114
Patriarchs 52, 61
persecution 14, 18, 22, 35, 37
Persia 166
Pilate 20, 21, 89, 94, 95
Pontius Pilate 21, 94, 95
Pope Innocent III 14
President Rivlin 164
Prinz, Hirsch 60
Promised Land 55-56, 76, 78, 102, 105, 113, 142, 176
prophecies 40-42, 44, 51, 59, 66, 70, 78, 114, 119, 121-123, 128, 138-139, 168, 170-171, 175

prophets 17, 20, 39, 40, 47, 72, 96, 109, 111, 113, 123, 126, 144, 151, 156, 162
Protocols of the Elders of Zion, The 16

R

rabbinic Judaism 152, 162
Rabbi Simeon ben Yochai 60, 62
Rambam 85
Rashi 42, 51, 85-88, 97, 118, 124
repentance 22, 87, 96, 100, 101, 104, 106-108, 124, 135, 152, 158, 174-175
resurrection 20, 32, 45, 57, 67, 91, 95-97, 111, 114, 119, 136, 160
Roman Catholicism 14, 23, 131
Rosenburg, Alfred 33
Russia 24, 165, 166, 170
Russian Orthodox Church 15, 24

S

Sabbath 11, 38, 92, 147-148, 153, 158, 176
Schneerson, Rabbi Menachem 37, 48
second coming 67, 120-122, 127-129, 134-138, 174, 176, 178
Seed of the Woman 79
Septuagint 69, 70
7 Laws of Noah 130, 131
70 AD 79, 100, 112, 115, 153
70 weeks 118
Sermon on the Mount 155
Shochet, Rabbi Immanuel 51
Simmons, Rabbi 142, 143, 144

Six Day War of 1967 166-167
Sodom 41, 53, 55, 122
Sodom and Gomorrah 41
Sokolovsky, Rabbi 44
Solomon's Temple 173
Spanish Inquisition 15
Spiro, Rabbi Ken 110-111
Suffering Servant 7, 45, 83, 97, 121, 126, 175
swastika 33
Syria 67, 73, 74, 78, 165, 166

T

Taliban 10
Talmud, 85, 118, 125
Targum 44, 64, 85
Targum of Palestine 136
Temple in Jerusalem 37, 39, 118, 165
Temple Mount 109
Temple Mount Faithful, The 109
Temple, the Second 7, 78, 109-110, 116, 118-119, 138, 152, 171
ten lost tribes 122
Tenach, the 42, 48, 50-51, 66, 107, 118-119, 127, 132, 146
Teutonic Master Race 32
tribulation 134, 135, 177
two-state solution 166

U

United Nations (UN) 41, 166, 170-171
universalism 131
universal peace 122-123, 127-128, 176
USA 50, 51, 170

Uzziel, Jonathan ben

V

virgin birth 7, 65-67, 70, 76-77, 79-81

W

Wagner's music 33
"War on Terrorism" 10
Western Wall 11
Wiesel, Elie 25, 26, 27, 28
Winston, Rabbi Pinchas 161-162, 165
witchcraft 132
world peace 37, 39, 47, 137, 139, 161, 168, 170, 173
World War II 118
Written Law 38, 144, 146, 152
Written Torah 38, 60, 143, 144, 145, 146, 152

Y

Yom Kippur 85, 101, 116, 118, 157, 159

Z

Zakkai, Rabbi Yohanan ben 100, 153
Zionism 110

To order additional copies of:
The Messiah Factor
Send $14.95 per book plus shipping to:
Lighthouse Trails Publishing
P.O. Box 908
Eureka, MT 59917
(U.S. Shipping is $3.95 for 1 book;
$5.25/2-3 books; $10.95/4-20 books)

You may also purchase Lighthouse Trails books from
www.lighthousetrails.com. For a complete listing of all Lighthouse Trails
resources, request a free catalog.

For bulk rates of 10 or more copies (40% off retail), contact Lighthouse Trails
Publishing, either by phone, e-mail, or fax. You may also order retail or bulk online
at www.lighthousetrails.com, or call our toll-free number:
866/876-3910 (USA/CA)
For international and all other calls:
406/889-3610
Fax: 406/889-3633

The Messiah Factor, as well as other books by Lighthouse Trails Publishing, can be
ordered through all major outlet stores, bookstores, online bookstores, and Christian
bookstores in the U.S. Bookstores may order through: Ingram, SpringArbor, Anchor,
or directly through Lighthouse Trails. Libraries may order through Baker & Taylor.

Visit our research site at www.lighthousetrailsresearch.com.

You may visit the author's website at:
https://lightforthelastdays.co.uk
You may contact the author at:
at:
Tony Pearce
Light for the Last Days
BM 4226
London
WC1N 3XX

To order *The Messiah Factor* in the UK,
contact the London address above. For UK orders, make checks out to
"Light for the Last Days" and allow 14 days for delivery.